The Revd Rebecca Kirkpatrick is a minister in the Presbyterian Church (USA). She currently serves as Associate Pastor for Adult Education and Mission at Bryn Mawr Presbyterian Church, Pennsylvania. She served for ten years as Associate Pastor for Education and Youth at Sunnyside Presbyterian Church, South Bend, Indiana. She blogs about Christian education and nurturing the spiritual lives of children at <www.breadnotstones.com>, where the list in this book first appeared.

100 THINGS FOR YOUR CHILD TO KNOW BEFORE CONFIRMATION

Growing faith together

Rebecca Kirkpatrick

First published in Great Britain in 2015

Society for Promoting Christian Knowledge
36 Causton Street
London SW1P 4ST
www.spck.org.uk

British Library Cataloguing-in-Publication Data
A catalogue record for this book is available from the British Library

ISBN 978–0–281–07298–9
eBook ISBN 978–0–281–07299–6

Typeset by Graphicraft Limited, Hong Kong
First printed in Great Britain by Ashford Colour Press
Subsequently digitally printed in Great Britain

eBook by Graphicraft Limited, Hong Kong

Produced on paper from sustainable forests

To Owen

Contents

Acknowledgements

In this book I acknowledge again and again the ways that seeds of faith planted in children and young people can, when nurtured and watered, fed and pruned, grow into a mature expression of faith. I am so grateful to those who mentored me in the faith as a child and young person and modelled for me what it means to teach and care for children as a community of faith – most importantly Judy Menk, who was not just my own confirmation teacher but who has become a colleague and friend.

In the many years that I have taught confirmation I have greatly valued the input of colleagues in ministry, who have been wonderful collaborators and conversation partners in the challenging work of nurturing faith in young people – most especially the Reverends Sarah Sanderson-Doughty, Shelly White Wood, Beth Freese Dammers and Anna Parkinson.

I have also been blessed to be able to partner in this work with gifted Christian educators. I would not be the pastor or the teacher I am today without the mentorship and friendship of both Jean Savage and Linda Linnen.

I am so grateful to my family for their support not just of this project but of all my writing and my work in ministry. I could not have written this book without the encouragement of my husband, Joshua Yoder. Thank you for your patience, your enthusiasm, your questions, your advice and of course your editing.

I am especially thankful for the encouragement of the Revd Mary Hawes and my commissioning editor at SPCK, Tracey Messenger. This book would not exist without their help and support.

Finally, I want to acknowledge all of the young men and women who spent countless hours in a classroom with me over the years talking about the Bible, the Church and what it means to live a life of faith. I am so grateful for your questions and your answers, your willingness to struggle with me and with faith, and your courage to express faith not just in class but with the community. The things you taught me are the greatest gift I have received in my ministry.

1

Growing a life of faith together

I can identify four moments from my teenage life that significantly changed how I understood the Bible and Christian faith. These four moments sparked within me a motivation to learn more about Scripture, to be engaged in my community and to seek out conversation partners on what has been a lifelong journey of faith.

The first came during confirmation when I finally noticed that the Bible contains no stories of Jesus' life as a teenager. I remember writing in my confirmation notebook, 'How am I supposed to relate to Jesus as a teenager when we don't know what it was like for *him* to be a teenager?' I knew the stories of Jesus' birth, his ministry, his death and his resurrection, but as a 13 year old it didn't seem like our lives had much in common. This was the first moment I remember that I really wanted to the Bible to be meaningful to *me*.

Around that same time I re-read the story of the Prodigal Son in the Gospel of Luke and for the first time understood it as theologically significant. I already knew the details well, having spent a week of theatre church camp cast in a musical version of the story. But it wasn't until I was a teenager that I understood the importance of the father's unqualified forgiveness and the desperation that the son felt. All of a sudden, what had seemed like a simple parable gave me language to describe the grace and love of God in a way that finally made sense to me.

A year or so later I had a similar experience, but this time at a large Presbyterian youth conference. In one of the worship services the Gospel lesson was the story of the woman at the well from the Gospel of John. In addition to the reading of the passage, a group of performers created a liturgical dance that retold the story of Jesus' encounter with this marginal woman. Up to that point I knew in my mind that Jesus had unique encounters and relationships with women, but it was only through this creative interpretation of this powerful story that I realized that maybe I, as a young woman, had a unique way to relate to Jesus.

Finally, in my later teen years my youth pastor told me there were parts of the Bible she really struggled with – especially the writings of Paul. Even though I knew who Paul was and knew that many of the letters in the New Testament were written by him, I had never read any of them closely enough to know how full they were of language that limited the authority of women. I was fascinated both by her frustration at the Bible and by her commitment to it nevertheless. No one had ever shared that with me before, and when I also came to struggle with the Bible, she served as a model for how a person can faithfully ask hard questions of the Scriptures.

I share these four epiphanies because they have two things in common that are essential in the spiritual development of our children and young people. First, each of these revelations was rooted in the Bible stories and church experiences that had been planted in me from a young age. Second, each occurred because of a connection I had to the adults in my community of faith – my Sunday-school teachers, my parents, my pastors, even the faithful and thoughtful leaders of that youth conference. Each of them took the time to nurture within me the tools I would need to deepen my faith, and each knew when the time was right to introduce me to a more sophisticated, more personal, maybe even more radical way of understanding the Bible and the Christian experience.

The confirmation experience

As a pastor in the Presbyterian Church (USA) for the past 12 years, it has been my great privilege to be a part of the same kinds of moments of growth and deepening of faith for young men and women.

In many instances these kinds of epiphanies happened within the context of confirmation class. In the Presbyterian Church students around the ages of 13 and 14 typically spend a year in preparation to confirm their baptism – or be baptized as an adult – and to become what we call an *adult* member of a local congregation. Because these classes are usually smaller than a regular Sunday-school class or youth event, they can be a fertile environment to nurture within young people a curiosity about the Bible and Christian faith and to provide a safe space to ask and even answer some of the questions about the Christian experience they have rolling around in their heads or weighing on their hearts.

The longer I worked with young people in these classes the more I noticed, year after year, that students were no longer coming to the class with the kinds of questions I had had, and were barely prepared to engage in any of the questions I placed before them.

Concerned that this was a symptom of our congregational life or our curriculum, I started asking colleagues in other churches and other traditions if they were having the same experiences. Indeed they were, and they were just as frustrated as I was becoming. For all of us, this year in which we had hoped and planned to help young people take an important next step in their journey of faith – connecting what they already knew from the Bible with their personal experience, learning how to ask faithful questions of the Bible and the Church and finding their place within the community celebrating the gifts they had to offer – was gradually turning instead into a remedial Sunday-school class where we rushed to try to pack in everything about the Church and the Bible they should have already learnt at an earlier age.

As a way to try to understand what it seemed students were missing and what basic knowledge I expected of them, I created a list of 100 things I would want them to know before they stepped into my confirmation class. This list became a tool for me as a pastor, for parents in our congregation and for our staff to assess what materials we were covering in our weekly Sunday school and how we were resourcing parents to be Christian educators within their homes. As I worked with the list, it also became a way to help parents better understand the progression of faith development their children can experience when they are nurtured in the faith from an early age.

It also served as fodder for conversations on my blog about how we teach the Bible to children and how even knowledge of the simplest of Bible stories can provide the seed of a new and deeper way for young people to connect with their faith.

That list has now become this book, which takes this conversation one step further, looking at the ways parents, leaders and educators within the church can see how each conversation, each lesson plan, each community activity, each moment in worship can build upon another to grow within young men and women a deep and curious faith.

A vision for Christian education

In my experience, effective Christian education – in the church or at home – should take students through progressive steps of knowledge and understanding as they grow:

- when they are children, exposing them to the essentials of Scripture, worship, and Christian life;
- then, as they get a little older, starting around the age of 12, teaching them skills for identifying patterns and traditions when we look at these Christian essentials as a whole;
- as they take on more responsibility for their religious identity, fostering within them an ability to think critically about faith and Scripture and, based on this critical thinking, to make an 'adult' decision to confirm their identity as a Christian;
- finally, as older teenagers walking beside them, studying Scripture on a deeper level and, having claimed an identity as a Christian, practising and learning what that means for who God has called them to be as well as how their faith informs their daily living.

It is at this critical third transitional step, when students are called upon to integrate what they already know about the Bible and Christianity into their personal identity (a step that in my tradition happens in the year-long confirmation preparation process), that we can most radically see the consequences of the holes that have crept in to our children's religious education.

When I first created the list of 100 things and presented it to the Christian Education Committee in my congregation and then to the parents of an incoming confirmation class, there were two reactions. First, there was a sense of being overwhelmed at all the things students should have as a foundation in their primary Christian education. Second, as people worked more closely with the list it became clear that it barely scratched the surface when it comes to the potential for biblical and Christian knowledge.

This book will not focus on the reasons why so many of us as parents and educators are seeing more and more of our children unprepared to take meaningful steps in their faith development as they reach their teen years. There are too many to count and too many that we cannot even hope to change.

- What we can do is be clearer about the basics we need to be teaching our children instead of just assuming they will pick them up along the way.
- What we can do is nurture parents in our congregations, giving them the tools, the education and the encouragement to be partners in their children's religious education.
- What we can do as parents is be more intentional about having real and honest conversations with our children about the Bible and our faith, without being worried that we don't know enough to be their teachers.
- What we can do is consider how each precious moment that we do have children in an educational setting at church can be a moment to work towards this larger goal of mature faith.
- What we can do is identify adult mentors within our churches who are willing to walk alongside young people as they grow into their faith, sharing models of Christian living and faithful curiosity.

It is my hope that this book will help us all to do each of these things better.

Growing faith

Number 75 in the list in this book is the Parable of the Mustard Seed from the Gospel of Matthew, in which Jesus speaks about faith and how much one needs to have – telling his disciples that even a small amount of faith, as small as a mustard seed, will be enough to move a mountain. Several years ago at the end of one of my most engaged confirmation classes, the students – and their parents – gave me a small charm on a necklace, a miniature phial containing a collection of mustard seeds. On the bottom of the phial they had engraved 'Planted 2009'.

It was a touching gift, and I do believe that among that group of young people, seeds of faith were planted that have continued to grow within them as they live into their adult faith beyond high school. But the truth is that we had fruitful conversations that year because of the seeds that were actually planted and fed in them for years before – even before I was their pastor. Seeds planted by their parents, their Sunday-school teachers, their grandparents, older teenagers in the congregation, and all the other people in their lives who encouraged their faith and made them feel like a welcomed part of the Christian community.

2

How to use this book

———————•◆•———————

This list of 100 Bible stories, characters, verses, church traditions, habits and conversations represents the foundational knowledge that I believe children and younger teenagers should have in order to make the transition to the next level of faith expression as older teenagers and young adults. The list is broken up topically, moving through the Old and New Testaments, worship practices, and then ten items at the end focusing on how Christians relate to one another and to the world.

You can read this book from cover to cover to get a sense of the breadth of information we should be teaching children, or it can serve as a reference tool for parents and educators as they look for additional support related to specific items.

The most important thing to keep in mind is that in almost all instances I am assuming that you will use this book alongside a Bible. There are too many stories packed into this list for me to be able to quote or summarize all of them. I do my best to mention details and highlights that relate specifically to the insights I share on each item, but I have also given you the specific book, chapter and verse each refers to so that you can do the work of reading these parts of the Bible on your own. This book and this list is not meant to replace or summarize biblical material but rather to help highlight some essentials for parents who are looking for a way to make teaching the Bible to children seem more manageable.

The second important thing to know is that each suggestion or interpretation I offer for each item is simply a starting point for conversations and interpretation. I am not offering a definitive interpretation of any part of the Bible but rather am giving examples of child-friendly ways to enter into conversations about Scripture when they are young and then more challenging ways we can study Scripture together with young people as they mature in their faith.

Most of the writing I do and the initial impetus for this list is to help parents gain a better sense of how to be an active part of their child's religious education. When I became a parent I began to realize that as a pastor I had the benefit of training and preparation that made having conversations with my son about faith, church and the Bible relatively second nature to me. But I also soon realized that what I was doing with my son at home was not really very complicated or beyond the reach of any parent. The problem is that we don't take the time to equip parents to do this work and to have these conversations. This book aspires to be a source of encouragement and empowerment for parents to take on this task.

It should also serve as a resource and tool for Christian educators in the congregational setting – both professional and volunteer. The list as a whole can be a way to spark conversations about what the essentials are in your context and can also be a tool for intentional conversations with parents about what children should be learning and how to spark these conversations across the generations.

Finally, this book can serve as an inspiration for parents and educators alike as we envision the religious potential for our children as they grow in their faith. While the goal in a moment like confirmation is to empower students to profess their faith in Jesus Christ publicly, we should also focus on a broader and more long-term goal of equipping them for a dynamic and curious Christian life.

For each item in the book, I reflect on and give ideas in three different areas:[1]

Planting the seed

These first sections are written mostly for parents and primarily for one-to-one conversations we can have with children as we introduce a variety of biblical stories and concepts, family traditions and Christian practices. Sometimes I have shared examples from my own conversations with my son, and sometimes I share my own struggles to teach these basics at home. Frequently these suggestions apply to more than just one item on the list but are general ideas for how to kick-start conversations on these topics with children.

---

[1] I group and discuss some items on the list together – such as, notably, the Ten Commandments but others too. Therefore you will not find individual 'Planting the seed', 'Feeding the soil' and 'Watching them grow' sections for every item on the list of 100.

Feeding the soil

These next sections address how we can nurture the seeds planted at home with parents in a congregational or community setting. Some of these ideas focus on larger issues of how we teach the Bible in the classroom setting. Others seek to be new ideas on standard Bible stories that can help to supplement existing teaching materials you are already using. Others again will challenge you to consider new topics on traditional Sunday-school lessons, or will consider how we teach children at church *outside* the classroom, in the ways through which they are introduced to and included in the larger life and work of the church. Some of these examples come from the traditions and programmes of the congregation I served for over ten years (2002–13) in South Bend, Indiana. Their willingness to engage children in the full life of the congregation and to experiment in the classroom helped to shape many of these innovative ideas.

Watching them grow

These last sections represent the potential next steps that young people can take in their faith as they build and expand on the concepts and practices planted in them at an earlier age. Most importantly, I have included some of the questions young people brought to me over the ten years that I taught confirmation class, as well as the questions I posed to them to try to expand the way they engaged with their faith and with the Bible.

As you move through this book and these different moments of growth and development you will note that I refer to different stages and ages in different ways. In order to be clear, here are the different groups of students to which I am typically referring:

- 'children' most often means from about age 3 to 11;
- 'younger children' typically refers to from age 3 to about 7;
- 'older children' means 8 through 11;
- 'young people' means 12 through 18 (which we typically refer to in my US context as 'youth');
- 'younger teenagers' will typically mean 12–14;
- 'older teenagers' will mean 15–18.

3

Bible basics

The best tool we can give our children at any point in their journey of faith is a Bible that fits their needs for that particular season of their life. As young people become more able to interact seriously with the Bible and how it shapes and challenges their faith, they need the right kind of Bible to help them feel confident in that work. In my experience that meant that at around 14 years of age, right as they are starting their confirmation preparation, we would give students a quality study Bible. A study Bible will have cultural and historical notes in the text, more detailed maps and thorough introductions to each individual book of the Bible. My two favourite study Bibles are the *HarperCollins Study Bible* and the *New Oxford Annotated Bible*.[1] I always point out to students that these are the Bibles I use myself to prepare to teach or preach, empowering them to think of themselves as capable of studying and wrestling with Scripture right alongside their pastor.

But a study Bible should not be the first Bible they ever read or even that they ever own. The majority of the 100 items listed in this book seek to increase students' biblical literacy in preparation for having the kind of deeper conversations about their faith that they will have as they mature. This happens best when they are regularly hearing, reading and talking about the stories of the Bible from an early age.

The first five items on this list focus primarily on *how* we approach reading the Bible with children and younger teenagers. Every time you read the Bible with children, each one of these five points can come into play and should be both in the back of your mind and on the tip of your tongue.

---

[1] *HarperCollins Study Bible: Student Edition, Fully Revised and Updated* (London: HarperCollins/ Society of Biblical Literature, 2006); *New Oxford Annotated Bible with Apocrypha: New Revised Standard Version* (Oxford: Oxford University Press, 2010).

1 The Bible is made up of many different books with different authors

This might seem obvious, but it is good to start with the most basic things. The Bible was compiled over centuries, as communities of faith recognized different writings to be both authentic and sacred. Different traditions recognize slightly different collections of writings, and some put those writings in a different order in the Bible.

Planting the seed

Sitting down for 15 minutes with a standard Bible in any translation, it is fairly easy to see that the Bible is actually a collection of multiple books. The problem is that we often don't sit down with a regular Bible and look at the table of contents with our children.

As a pastor I always tell people that I am in the Bible distribution business and am happy to give Bibles to any child who needed one, regardless of their place in our community. But as we make our way through this list, parents should remember that they are in the Bible 'teaching' business with their children. If your church does not have a tradition of giving Bibles to children, it is not hard to find one to give them yourself. If your child does not own their own – non-picture book – Bible, take this first step and buy them their own today. There are a few different things to keep in mind when choosing the right Bible for your child, including the particular translation and the in-text notes that help children think more deeply about different stories. For me, the in-text notes are the most valuable thing to consider, especially when I am sitting down to read with my ten-year-old son. The best children's Bible for that right now is the *Deep Blue Bible*.[2]

Most children's Bibles have an introduction at the start of each individual book giving a brief explanation of what it is about, who we think may have written it and themes that readers should be on the lookout for. It is always worth the time to take the extra five minutes to read that introduction with children before you read a passage or story in any particular book.

---

[2] *CEB Deep Blue Kids Bible* (Nashville, TN: Common English Bible, 2012).

Feeding the soil

The congregation I served traditionally gave children around six years old a substantial picture Bible – one organized like a Bible and covering the majority of the stories included in my list of 100. By the time students are eight or nine, it is clear they are ready for a regular Bible. Some are ready earlier than that.

But this didn't mean that children brought those Bibles with them to Sunday school week to week. No matter what incentives we tried, nothing could help establish that habit. Every time you gather to teach children you should have enough Bibles in the room for each child to be able to look up whatever passage is being taught that day. It is not good enough for the leader to just pass their Bible to one child to read out loud from. Every child, *every week*, needs to have an opportunity to look up a passage from the Bible; through that regular practice, the organization of the Bible will become second nature to them.

Watching them grow

As students get older they progress from the concept of different books and different authors to talking about the different types of literature found in the Bible – histories, laws, wisdom, prophets, letters and poetry, to name a few.

- How do we read a psalm differently from a genealogy?
- Who decided what books should be in the Bible?
- Where did all these books come from?
- Who were these people who wrote the Bible and how do we know that what they wrote is true?[3]

2 Much of the Bible comes from ancient oral tradition

We should remind children and young people that we tell the stories of the Bible because generations of people before us have told these stories about God. Even before they were written down, people made sure to tell the stories to one another so that they had a way to

---

[3] For more on questions and topics beyond the scope of this book, see Appendix 2, Further reading, at the end.

understand God together. This applies to the stories in the New Testament as well, since we know that stories about Jesus were told for at least a generation after his death before the Gospels we have in the Bible today were written down.

Planting the seed

It is not uncommon for my son, after reading a particularly strange or scary story from the Bible, to turn to me and ask if I believe it really happened. The first time he asked me this I chose my words very carefully. I told him that I believe that ancient people who lived a long time ago really told this story to each other as they tried to understand who God was for them. I told him that I believe that the story, when we read it in the Bible and when we tell it to each other again, helps us understand who God is for us today.

Children can be just as fascinated with the ancient world of Mesopotamia as they are with ancient Egypt, Rome or Greece, if we foster that kind of curiosity in them. As much as we want them to feel that the Bible is relevant for them as modern people, we also need to instil in them a sense of the antiquity of these stories. That means reminding them that parts of the Bible and its stories are so old that the only way people had of preserving them was by telling them to each other over and over again.

Feeding the soil

In a classroom setting we should always root the stories and traditions of the Bible in the ancient culture and geography in which they were written. While children may not be ready to study the Bible as comparative literature, they should be able to understand that it is an epic story, just like other epic stories told by ancient people.

A benchmark I like to use when writing or adapting a lesson plan is to ask myself whether or not I am teaching a younger child something I will have to correct when they are older. For example, while I might refer to the first five books of the Bible as the Books of Moses, I never tell children that authorship of these books was traditionally attributed to Moses. Modern biblical scholarship has clearly disproved this theory. This also means being meticulous in selecting and reviewing classroom materials and adapting them when necessary.

Watching them grow

As we explore the Bible with older teenagers we have time to read stories more closely than students will ever have done before. A close and holistic reading of the Bible reveals repetitions, conflicting versions and competing instructions. When students come to these conversations already understanding that the Bible is the product of generations of telling and retelling – not a book that dropped out of the clouds one day as a gift from God – they can look at some of these more interesting passages and ask questions about how the differences can inform and inspire our faith.

A foundational question to introduce is the difference between 'facts' and 'truth' when it comes to the Bible. We can explore what it means that the Bible has been inspired by God over generations and how we can understand its importance as a guiding influence for our life of faith today.

3 The Old Testament is the story of the Israelite people

Students know that Christians trace their roots through the Jewish tradition, and they know that there are still Jewish people today, but sometimes they don't make the connection that we share these stories; that they were – and still are – Jewish stories before they were Christian stories.

Planting the seed

You should start every conversation about a story from the Bible by either asking children or pointing out to them which part of the Bible it comes from. If you are helping them to learn to use the table of contents in their Bible, it is very easy to point out that the story they are reading may come from the first part of the Bible called – by Christians – the Old Testament. These are the stories of the Jewish people that all took place before Jesus was born. These are the stories of Jesus' ancestors. These are the Bible stories he would have known as a child, a youth and an adult. As I move through the rest of the Old Testament items in this list I will help you know how to describe the different stages of this larger story to children, so that even though they are focusing on details, they will eventually come away with a larger understanding of the story of Israel.

Feeding the soil

Maps are wonderful tools to help children understand the Bible. A world map puts into perspective the location on the globe where the stories in the Bible take place in relation to where we live today, but sometimes the most effective map is very detailed and focused on just one story from the Bible. Class time can also be spent in teaching children how to use the maps located at the back of most Bibles. Whether it is a modern or ancient map, children should be taught how to find Israel and other major landmarks from the Old Testament. For children who are visual learners, this simple addition to studying the Bible makes it that much more real and significant to them.

Watching them grow

Older students should be ready to talk about the larger themes of the Old Testament: monotheism, covenant, liberation, atonement, the Temple, messianic expectations and exile.

- How does the Old Testament describe God?
- How does it present God as a character in the lives of the ancient Israelites?
- How does that God compare to the neighbouring gods of other ancient cultures when we read more obscure passages in the Old Testament like Leviticus 20.1–5, which speaks of the god Molech who was said to require child sacrifice?

Over the years my confirmation students always had questions about why God seems so different in the Old Testament compared to the New Testament. This is a great example of the kind of conversation that can take place only if a student has already been exposed to enough of the Bible, shown that there are two major sections – Old and New – and had time to start asking more complicated questions about what they are being taught. When I have had students reach the age of 14 with no sense that God is portrayed in different ways in different stories (let alone that those portrayals are characteristic relative to the part of the Bible in which we find them), the majority of time I have in class with them is spent introducing the concept, with little left for the possibility of 'problematizing' it and then resolving questions students may have.

4 The New Testament is the story of the life of Jesus and the early Christians

The Gospels tell the story of Jesus' life. The book of Acts, the letters of Paul and all of the other New Testament literature teach us the stories of the Early Church and early Christian theology. I will go into much more detail on helping children learn to navigate through the New Testament in items 41–80.

Planting the seed

The same techniques used when reading the Old Testament can apply to reading the New. Children's picture Bibles are notoriously neglectful when it comes to including New Testament stories or passages beyond the Gospels (or rather, the amalgamation of the four Gospels that we teach to children). Simply pointing out to children, as you read stories of Jesus together, that they are a part of the New Testament is a great first step in helping them orientate themselves within their Bible.

It is not uncommon for Christians to look for signs or connections to Jesus Christ when they read the Old Testament. Certainly to understand Jesus of Nazareth as the Messiah written of in the Old Testament means that there are many legitimate connections to be made. I would caution, though, against some children's Bibles that do biblical acrobatics to find connections. Sometimes there are connections, and certainly there are *many* connections to be made to the Old Testament when reading the New with children.

As you move through the rest of this book and the list, I will give you examples of the legitimate connections that can easily be taught to your children when you are talking with them about the Bible.

Feeding the soil

Just as maps are great tools to use in teaching the Bible to children, biblical timelines are also a great way to help illustrate the story and the stories of the Bible. On a biblical timeline children can see the difference in time between the stories of the Old Testament, which span over a thousand years, and those of the New Testament, which take place in less than a hundred. Again, visual learners will appreciate this kind of presentation of the Bible as they try to wrap their heads around the thousands of years it covers. If you have a dedicated room in which you teach, post the timeline permanently there and have the children add an arrow or sticker to it on the spot where that day's story would be found. Some timelines are very portable – if yours is you can also bring it out as a regular resource for children to use. Each week, just as one volunteer finds the story in the Bible another can find its place on the timeline.[4]

Watching them grow

Students growing into their identity as Christians can learn in more depth about the development of Christianity in the first century and about the early Christian community. To be able to do that, they should come with a basic understanding of the New Testament.

- What does it mean for them to declare for themselves that Jesus Christ is their Lord and Saviour?
- What does it mean to be part of a 2,000-year-old tradition?

5 There are many different modern translations of the Bible

The Bible was written originally in Hebrew and Greek, so clearly any Bible in English is going to be a translation. Depending on your tradition, you may prefer to teach your child from one translation rather than another, or your church may have a preference.

Planting the seed

It is highly likely that the Bible you already own as an adult – maybe one you recently bought, the Bible you were given as a child or teenager, or even one you inherited from your own parents or grand-parents – is a different translation from the one your child has been given.

Choose one of your favourite passages or stories and read it to-gether with your child from both translations. This can be especially

---

[4] In the UK, Scripture Union produce a 16-panel Bible timeline aimed at children aged 8–11; see Victoria Beech and Matt Baker (illus.), *Bible Timeline: Bible History at a Glance* (Milton Keynes: Scripture Union, 2012). A cheaper mini-version is also available.

fun if you have a King James Version of the Bible. While I myself prefer a more modern translation, there are some parts of Scripture that are absolutely beautiful in that Elizabethan style. Ask your child to help point out the differences in translation and how they think it might change the meaning of the verse or story.

Feeding the soil

The chances are also very high that within your church you have cupboards stuffed with older translations of the Bible that no one knew what to do with when new ones were purchased. Inevitably our Sunday-school classrooms always had an eclectic collection of modern translations that would be passed out for children and young people to use during a lesson. It doesn't take long for students to realize that they are following along in different translations. On several occasions I have had students who would normally baulk at reading aloud from the Bible in class ask if they could share the translation they were using so that their classmates could hear the difference. This is just a simple way of building within students an awareness of the complexity of reading the Bible as modern people.

Watching them grow

In my confirmation class I always make sure to bring copies of the Hebrew and Greek texts to at least one meeting so students can get a sense of the foreignness of the Bible. We talk about how different translations can serve different purposes – study, devotion and so on – and how for those who are not able to read the Bible in the original languages, using multiple translations can help us think differently about what a passage might mean by hearing it in different ways.

4

The stories of Genesis and Exodus

When it comes to taking young people to the next step in reading and understanding the Bible, our task is twofold. First, we look more closely at some of these stories to appreciate their beauty and pay attention to the details. Second, we discuss what they teach us about who God is and about who we are as people who claim these stories as our own.

The practice of hearing and telling these stories throughout their lives helps children and then teenagers think of them as their stories, their tradition, their history. These stories from Genesis and Exodus are foundational for understanding the rest of the Bible, for identifying themes that appear throughout Scripture and for perceiving the allusions to them in much of the New Testament.

6 Creation and other primeval stories (Genesis 1—11)

I am already cheating when it comes to how this list is numbered, and this one item really includes several of the stories from the first several chapters of Genesis, representing an ahistorical pre- or primeval history.

In the story of the creation from Genesis 1.1—2.1a, God creates new elements of the earth each day; each day is good; and God rests on the last, the seventh day. In Genesis 3, God creates the first human beings – Adam and Eve – and places them in the Garden of Eden with the instruction not to eat of the tree of the knowledge of good and evil. But they eat and are banished from the garden as a punishment for their disobedience.

In Genesis 4 we read about Cain and Abel – the first two siblings and the first act of violence. Genesis 11 tells the story of the Tower of Babel, providing a narrative explanation for the existence of different cultures and languages.

Planting the seed

Start cultivating a cache of talking points or open-ended discussion starters that can help you teach your children how to ask questions of the Bible and how to handle questions that are unanswerable. They can be as simple as:

- What do you think about this story?
- What do you think this story teaches us about God?
- What does this story teach us about people?
- How does this story makes you feel?
- What do you like in this story and what do you not like?

The goal of these questions is not to find correct answers but teach children how to be curious about Scripture.

Feeding the soil

Children's Sunday-school materials do a pretty good job at covering most of these early biblical stories. The only one from this group frequently missing is the story of Cain and Abel. The very best resource I have ever used to teach this story to children is Rabbi Sandy Eisenberg Sasso's book *Cain & Abel: Finding the Fruits of Peace.*[1] It is written in the style of Jewish midrash, adding details and motivations to the biblical version. The book encourages children to think more specifically about what it means to hurt each other. A great strategy in using this book in the classroom would be to have children read the biblical version of the story first and then, as they are reading Sasso's, to point out the things that are similar to and different from the Bible.

Watching them grow

When students know the story of creation in the first chapter in Genesis, they can read the second story of creation in Genesis 2 and talk about the ways the two are different. In those conversations we talk about reading the Bible as a theological textbook not as a scientific textbook. We can have a discussion about original sin.

---

[1] Sandy Eisenberg Sasso and Joani Keller Rothenberg (illus.), *Cain & Abel: Finding the Fruits of Peace* (Woodstock, VT: Jewish Lights, 2001).

- Do we blame Adam and Eve or do we see ourselves in them?
- Do we pity Cain or do we understand that it is possible to sin against God and against one another?

7 Noah's Ark (Genesis 6—9)

This part of Genesis tells the story of Noah and his family's obedience to God in the midst of an otherwise irredeemable society. God chooses Noah and his family to preserve all the animals of the earth by building a large boat to house them. After 40 days of rain the flood slowly begins to subside. God renews his covenant with humanity, and through the sign of the rainbow promises never to destroy the earth by flood again.

Planting the seed

Even though it is often marketed as such, the story of Noah and the flood is not really one for young children. Don't feel pressured to read this story together with your child too soon. While there are many beautiful artistic interpretations of this story for young children, there are many adult themes that are often overlooked when the story is paraphrased.

Be careful not to get too caught up in children's questions of scale:

- How could that many animals fit on one boat?
- How did they keep the carnivores from eating the other animals?
- How could there be that much water on the earth?

Instead, help children focus on the faithful response of Noah and the way God makes a covenant with him and his descendants at the end.

Feeding the soil

The same question of *why* that we – and children – want to ask when confronted with such a difficult story of devastation is also the one we ask any time a natural disaster strikes in our world today. Use the study of Noah and his faithful response to God to introduce children and your faith community to the many disaster-relief organizations that work together to respond when crisis strikes around the world. While we often respond as communities after the fact, the truth is that many organizations need year-round financial and material support to help them be prepared to respond at a moment's notice.

For example, some in the USA encourage donations of 'clean-up buckets' that can help individuals and families start the recovery process. Use a sample bucket in the classroom to talk together about what it is like to move on after a disaster, just like Noah and his family had to, or get hold of some other fundraising materials from charities such as WaterAid, which works to provide clean water and sanitation for those in greatest need.[2]

Watching them grow

When students are older, the story of Noah helps us talk about several biblical themes: sin, punishment, forgiveness and covenant. Does God really need a reminder not to destroy the earth? Should we make a connection between natural disasters and the wrath of God, or is God more forgiving than before? These questions don't have easy answers, but raising them in class helps students learn how to ask hard questions about Bible stories.

8 Abraham and Sarah (Genesis 12—23)

The tales of Abraham and Sarah span much of Genesis but can be narrowed down for both children and young people to just a few key events. First there is the general story of Abraham's call and God's covenant with him. This story repeats throughout, but the key theme is that God promises to give Abraham land and many descendants. In one instance God tells him that these descendants will be as numerous as the stars. In another, three visitors come to Abraham and Sarah, who are quite old at this point, and announce that Sarah will bear a son they will name Isaac. Finally is the sacrifice – or, as some call it, the 'binding' – of Isaac in Genesis 22.

Planting the seed

The stories of God's promises to Abraham and Sarah can help introduce children to the concept of a 'family of faith'. As you read of God making Abraham's descendants as numerous as the stars, point out to your children that they are counted among those stars. Abraham's family is bigger than his biological family, and includes all of the people who have worshipped God in the past and still worship God today.

---

[2] See <www.wateraid.org>.

Feeding the soil

One of the elements of the larger epic of Abraham and Sarah that is overlooked when we skip from story to story is all of the travel that this ancient couple did at the request of God. We tell children that Abraham was faithful because he left his home behind and travelled to where God called him.

Bring out a map of Canaan and Egypt to show how far he had to go. Help children talk about what it would mean to pack up everything you owned and leave behind everything you knew. Assign the different passages that describe Abraham and Sarah's travel to different children and ask them to work together to trace their journey.

Watching them grow

These stories help to introduce the biblical themes of call and covenant. God calls us to do difficult things we sometimes feel unequipped for. Abraham and Sarah are a model for what it means to take a leap of faith. Young people can then use what they already know about God's promises to Abraham and Abraham's willingness to obey God to think together about the sacrifice of Isaac. Often when I work through these difficult stories with older teenagers, we look together at several artistic interpretations of the story, and there are many in various styles. By talking about the ways the artist imagines the scene and expresses the emotions of the characters, students can share their own impressions and reactions to a hard story. I believe it is also appropriate as students get older for them to hear from the adults in their lives that they too struggle with the Bible. I don't know any parent who doesn't flinch at reading this story.

9 Isaac and Rebecca (Genesis 24—27)

We come to the stories of Isaac and his wife Rebecca. Students can be taught to trace the family tree of Abraham through Joseph: Abraham begat Isaac who begat Jacob, who begat Joseph. Isaac and Rebecca have twin boys, Jacob and Esau. Jacob steals Esau's birthright twice, and is forced to flee from his home and the wrath of his brother.

Planting the seed

There are many stories of sibling rivalries in the Bible but these stories of Jacob and Esau – Genesis 25 and 27 – really are the most interesting and vivid. How often do our own children tempt each other, take advantage of each other, bargain with each other and even lie to their parents to get one over on each other? As much as these stories are steeped in ancient culture, they are totally relatable to today's children and young people.

It is poignant to read ahead with children to Genesis 33, which tells the story of Jacob and Esau's reunion when, as adults and heads of their own young families, the two brothers embrace and reconcile. How often do we try to assure our children that though they may struggle with their siblings today, their relationships as adults have the potential to be very different?

Feeding the soil

One of the larger goals of teaching the stories of the patriarchs and matriarchs of the Old Testament to children is to help them develop a larger understanding of what it means for someone to be an ancestor of faith. One way to do this, around Christmas, is to introduce the concept of the Jesse tree.

A Jesse tree uses symbols representing the heroes of faith and helps to link them together as they culminate in the life of Jesus Christ. The book of Isaiah says that a root will spring from the stump of Jesse (David's father), which is where the name originates. The first symbols added to the tree are always Abraham, symbolized by a star, Sarah, symbolized by a tent, Isaac, by a bundle of sticks reminiscent of his near sacrifice, and Rebecca, by a water jug reminding us of her meeting with Isaac's servant at the well.[3]

Watching them grow

To read these stories together allows us to talk about the nature of marriage and families in the Bible, of betrothal and inheritance, and of betrayal.

- What do we mean when we talk about biblical family values?
- Are there biblical marriages that reflect what we would strive for in a modern marriage?

---

[3] My all-time favourite template for creating a Jesse tree can be found in Martha Bettis Gee, *Things to Make & Do for Advent & Christmas* (Louisville, KY: Bridge Resources, 1997).

10 Jacob and his sons (Genesis 28—50)

The most critical parts of Jacob's larger story are his dream of a ladder to heaven with angels ascending and descending; Jacob wresting with the angel and receiving the name Israel; and the story of Jacob's sons who go on to represent the 12 tribes of Israel. This would also include the familiar stories of Joseph, the favoured son who is sold by his brothers into slavery, of his rise in the Egyptian court and then his eventual reconciliation with his brothers.

Planting the seed

One of the best places to focus conversation with children is towards the end of the story, in Joseph's statement to his brothers as he reveals himself to them in Egypt when they come looking for assistance during the famine. He tells them that even though the pain they caused him was bad, God has used his suffering for good. When have you or your family found good or hope in a difficult situation? While we don't want to claim that God gives us trials to test us, talk with children about how God stays with us through struggles and helps us find a way to be useful to the world even in a bad situation.

Feeding the soil

Again, these stories provide us with a wonderful visual aid to help children better understand both biblical themes and their biblical heritage. Jacob is given a new name by God, and his sons and grandsons become the 12 tribes: Benjamin, Judah, Naphtali, Zebulon, Issachar, Gad, Ruben, Levi, Simeon, Dan, Asher, Ephraim and Manasseh.

Work with children to understand these 12 tribes. Which tribe did Moses belong to (Exod. 2.1)? Saul (1 Sam. 9.1)? David (1 Sam. 16.1)? Look together at a map to see the locations where the different tribes settled when they entered the Promised Land. Point out that members of the tribe of Levi were called to be priests at the Temple, so they were never given their own land to settle. Deuteronomy 33 recounts the blessings Moses gave each tribe when they entered the Promised Land.

Watching them grow

When students already know the stories of these men and brothers, they can expand their biblical knowledge by learning the stories of the women from these lengthy narratives: Rachel and Leah (Gen. 29 and 30), Dinah (34) and Tamar (38).

11 The birth of Moses (Exodus 2)

In the first chapter of Exodus we are given background information to help us understand that the entire Israelite people have lived and prospered in Egypt but have in this generation fallen out of favour with the new king and are living there as slaves. Exodus 2 begins the story of Moses, born at a time when, to reduce the Hebrew population, all male boys are to be killed in infancy. Moses is hidden by his mother, set adrift in the Nile in a lined basket and rescued by the daughter of the king and raised as an Egyptian.

Planting the seed

Babies are very vulnerable people in the Bible, and it seems like bad things are always happening to them. The slaughter of the Hebrew boys will not be the first or last time you have to confront this issue when reading the Bible with your children. While we may be tempted to gloss over it or to avoid these stories altogether, it is worth reading them with children and showing them how we mourn the loss of innocent life, thousands of years ago and yet still today.

Feeding the soil

There are certain stories in the Bible that really seem to connect with children and stay firmly in their memory – and this story of Moses in the bulrushes is one of them. In these instances we start the process of broadening the biblical story for children. Reteaching or reviewing the birth of Moses in the classroom means we can introduce children to the story of Shiphrah and Puah, the Hebrew midwives who disobeyed the orders of the pharaoh and saved the lives of countless babies (Exod. 1.15). There are so many unnamed women in the Bible, and it is not clear why the names of these two women have been preserved. Their courage is worth teaching to children to expand their understanding of the world into which Moses was born and their definition of biblical heroes.

Watching them grow

Older students should start to notice patterns and themes repeated throughout the Bible. For example, we can look together at the connections between the birth of Moses and the stories of Jesus' birth found in the Gospel of Matthew: the threat against newborn boys and the flight into Egypt. This helps students remember that the first Christians, most of whom were Jewish, would have also known the stories of Moses by heart and immediately recognized the similarities.

12 The call of Moses (Exodus 3)

Moses, having fled Egypt as a young man, is living as a shepherd in Midian. One day while tending sheep he comes across a bush that is on fire but is not consumed. The voice of God speaks to him from the bush, telling Moses that he has heard the voice of his people crying out for liberation from their oppression from Egypt and is calling Moses to be the agent of that liberation.

Planting the seed

God has asked Moses to go and stand up for people who cannot stand up on their own. Even though Moses feels ill-equipped to take on that role, God promises him that he will have others in his life who will support him in this call. Younger children can be reminded that they should always look out for ways to help their friends and to stick up for people who are being picked on or who are pushed aside by others. Older children can be taught to think about the ways our calling as Christians is to care for the vulnerable in the world.

Feeding the soil

One of the most evocative elements of this story is not just the burning bush but the idea that by God's presence this random hill has been transformed into holy ground. Take children on a tour of your church building and sanctuary and talk about what makes a place holy.

- Is worship space holy because this is where we come to meet God?
- Is one space of the sanctuary more sacred than another?
- Where else do we meet God?
- Aren't those places holy as well, such as the classroom where we learn about God, places where we meet and spend time together, the kitchen where meals may be cooked to serve to the homeless in the community?
- What places are holy to them?

Watching them grow

As they contemplate their calling as adult Christians, students can delve deeper into the theme of call in the Bible – God revealing promises and plans; human beings often trying to cry off or questioning the wisdom of God's choice of them; God's self-revelation to those being called, giving them a vision of who God truly is. We talk about how we hear God today. How does God speak to us and call us to serve? Obviously it is not through burning bushes – so how can we be open to the call of God in our lives in more subtle ways?

13 The plagues (Exodus 7—12)

Moses returns to Egypt and negotiates for the release of the Israelites so that they can return to the land God has promised them in Canaan. The pharaoh does not agree and so God subjects him to a series of plagues to try to change his mind: water turned to blood; gnats; flies; death of livestock; boils; hail; locusts; darkness; and finally the death of the first born. It is this final plague that secures their release, at least temporarily.

Planting the seed

A friend once asked for advice on teaching this story to young children at their synagogue in a way that would not induce nightmares. I told her that having taught these stories to countless children, I never remember any one of them being any more scared than they were watching almost any cartoon. Actually I think the movies are scarier. I am not saying that this story is great for bedtime, but it is not as scary as some.

What is even scarier for children can be encountering these stories on their own. Even though it may be hard to imagine, there will be moments when children explore the Bible on their own. In those moments, encountering these truly difficult stories can cause confusion and misunderstandings over what the Bible is all about. This is why some of these hard yet foundational stories are important to read intentionally together with children so that they can ask questions and learn that struggling to understand the Bible is normal.

Feeding the soil

Often we ask children to memorize certain passages of Scripture, names of disciples, books of the Bible, prayers or even creeds. In an attempt to spice up these kinds of challenges, memorizing the plagues of the Exodus provides a creative way to try to engage students who find these tasks mindless or frustrating. This is such a vivid story as well, so it is a way to provide a challenge for students who are visual and narrative learners.

Watching them grow

The stories of the plagues are a starting point for understanding how God works in the world. While we try to teach that God works in the world for good and that natural disasters are not the movement of the hand of God, there are still these kinds of biblical stories that force us to face the idea of God's wrath and the power of God's anger. Do we just ignore the parts of the Bible that make us uncomfortable? Jumping ahead in Exodus, I always like to share with students the story of Moses angrily confronting God when God threatens to abandon the Israelites in the desert. If God can be angry at us, are we allowed to be angry at God?

14 The Exodus (Exodus 12—13)

The Israelites gather up all the possessions they can carry and flee together to the Red Sea, while the pharaoh sends his army to pursue them. Moses cries out to God and is given the power to part the sea so that they can cross over on dry ground. The pharaoh's charioteers follow on their heels. The waters descend, drowning them and assuring the escape of God's people.

Planting the seed

Within this story we can read of the establishment of the Festival of Unleavened Bread, which Jews came to call the Passover. While I think that it is disingenuous when Christians 'celebrate' a Passover feast, one of the things that is so beautiful about that particular Jewish holiday is that it is celebrated at home around the table and among the family.

Talk with Jewish friends who celebrate Passover and ask if there is a way for them to share their traditions with your children. I am not advocating inviting yourself to someone else's religious holiday, but if they have children of their own, find a time to be together as families and ask *their* children to teach and show *your* children how they celebrate the Passover together.[4]

Feeding the soil

Any time we are teaching children about the Last Supper and the institution of the Eucharist, we remind children why Jesus and his disciples were gathered for dinner that night. Gather children around a table to share unleavened bread and to read the story of the first Passover. Later on in this list I will talk about how we teach children about the Jewish roots of our Christian faith – see item 79. Instilling this concept in children helps them to understand some of the earliest struggles in the Early Church when they are older.

Watching them grow

This liberating moment, bringing the destruction of the Egyptian army, provides fodder for discussion about the Bible's message of freedom for God's people. We can ask who in our world is in need of liberation – from poverty, from oppression, from illness – and how Christians can help in that liberating work. This is also a great moment to talk about the significance the story of the Exodus has had for the African American Christian community. Many African American spirituals drew on themes from Exodus and the Old Testament – we can use a song like 'Go Down, Moses' to imagine what it would be like to be a slave in the world today and to know that God is a God of freedom.

15 *The wilderness experience* *(Exodus 15 and beyond)*

The Israelites go on to spend 40 years wandering in the wilderness of the Sinai, driving each other crazy, complaining to God and Moses, making some big mistakes and learning important lessons. Key stories are God giving the law to Moses on the top of Mount

---

[4] There are also many resources available to help parents and leaders learn more about Jewish holiday traditions, such as Yechiel Eckstein, *How Firm a Foundation: A Gift of Jewish Wisdom for Christians and Jews* (Brewster, MA: Paraclete Press, 1997).

Sinai, the creation of the Golden Calf and the giving of bread and water in the wilderness by God.

Planting the seed

One of my favourite aspects of these stories of the wandering of the Israelites in the wilderness is the unfiltered complaining they do all the time. Criticizing Moses for freeing them from slavery just so they can die in the wilderness; constantly complaining of hunger; desperate for water; unable to entertain themselves without getting in trouble. It sounds like a typical family excursion. I just love how we can read the Bible thousands of years later and hear in the echoes of these stories something we might have said – or yelled – at each other just yesterday.

When you read the Bible with children, take the time to point out these things that are so similar to our lives today.

- Can they think of situations in which they have reacted in the same way or with the same sentiment?
- Can they make the connections to situations they have been in when they have felt out of control, bored, hungry or tired?
- How easy was it to relieve their suffering?
- How hard would it have been for Moses to deal with these grumpy travellers?

Feeding the soil

When my son watched the DreamWorks film *The Prince of Egypt* as a young child, the very first thing he said at the end of the film was, 'They left out some of the best parts!' What he meant was that while the movie centred around the act of liberating the Israelites from Egypt, it glossed over almost the entirety of these stories of the people wandering lost in the wilderness. Yes, you see Moses receive the Ten Commandments, but there is little else representing the next 40 years of trials and struggles the people endured before they made it to the Promised Land.

We are all limited in the amount of time we have to teach children the stories of the Bible at church, and each time we choose to focus in on one story we have to sacrifice another. Even in creating this list of essentials, I was forced to abandon much-beloved stories for the sake of time and space.

The story of the Exodus is so epic that it is hard to make decisions about what to keep and what to set aside. How does your education programme encourage parents and children to read the Bible together at home? When studying the book of Exodus at church, give families readings to do together at home, making sure they are covering the sections you cannot in class. This way parents can be engaged in what their children are learning, stories and concepts are reinforced at home and they get a fuller picture of the entire Exodus narrative.

Watching them grow

When students come with an understanding of the trials that came after liberation, we can wrestle with the truth that with freedom comes struggle, with community come mistakes and with new laws – the Ten Commandments – come the inevitable moments when they are broken. The stories of God giving manna from heaven can inform our conversations about the bounty of Communion, and the water springing forth from the rock connects to the water stories throughout Scripture.

5

The Ten Commandments

In the course of teaching confirmation students I will often have them brainstorm a list of sins. Inevitably the first sin they name is swearing/taking the Lord's name in vain. I am not sure if this speaks to their general lack of personal experience as sinners in the world, the black and white nature of either swearing or not swearing or the reality that teaching our kids not to swear is the last bastion of human decency that we hope to pass on to them (at least while they are still young teenagers). Maybe it is my life experience or the many layers of grey that I have discovered in my own potential for sin that makes me chuckle each time they put swearing at the top of their list. After more discussion, and prompted by their knowledge of the Ten Commandments, we do get to the bigger sins – such as murder, lying, stealing.

Here is a paraphrase of the Ten Commandments as found in both the books of Exodus and Deuteronomy. They are numbers 16–25 in our list of 100, but I have primarily numbered them here in the traditional way to avoid confusion (followed by their number in the 100 list).

1 [16] You shall worship God alone
2 [17] You shall not make any idols of God
3 [18] You shall not abuse the name of God
4 [19] You shall keep the Sabbath holy
5 [20] Honour your father and mother
6 [21] You shall not murder
7 [22] You shall not commit adultery
8 [23] You shall not steal
9 [24] You shall not lie
10 [25] You shall not covet what your neighbour owns

Planting the seed

Teach children the story of God meeting Moses on Mount Sinai and teaching him the laws the people were to follow (Exod. 20 and 32). What could be better than the image of Moses carrying these two heavy stone tablets down to the people, only to discover them breaking Commandments 1 and possibly 2 already? Then he smashes the tablets to pieces – how exciting!

It is pretty easy to teach children about the Ten Commandments. The struggle is figuring out how we can teach our children actually to follow them.

I teach my child not to steal by telling him that stealing is wrong, and by not stealing myself. I teach him not to covet his neighbour's possessions through the painful conversations we wind up having at the end of a friend's birthday party. I teach him to honour me and his father in the way we honour our own parents, and by making sure there are consequences for disrespectful behaviour. I teach him to honour the Sabbath and keep it holy by making sure that worshipping with our faith community trumps any other commitment in our lives.

The key is to not just to teach our children that murder and envy, lying and worshipping false gods and so on are wrong, but also to teach them that the Bible puts a list of these all together for us to obey as followers of this one God.

Feeding the soil

When we establish rules for our Sunday-school classes we often engage children and young people in an exercise to help them create not just a behavioural covenant for the class but to foster a level of 'buy-in' to the rules for the class. Kick off this kind of activity with children by looking together first at the Ten Commandments, asking them to find ways that these ancient rules can be translated into classroom rules today.

A conversation about what it means to keep a holy Sabbath can lead to a covenant to value the time we share together as a community on the Lord's Day. A conversation about not murdering can lead to a covenant that we do not physically harm one another in the classroom. A conversation about not coveting our neighbours' possessions can ensure that we include a covenant to respect each other's personal space and each other's belongings.

Watching them grow

Young people who have grown up knowing and thinking about the Ten Commandments individually can then start looking at them more holistically. First, we can break them down into the two groups 1–4 and 5–10: sins against God and sins against one another. Which is worse? Which do we need more forgiveness for, and whose forgiveness do we need to ask for?

Second, we can move from that conversation to an introduction of the *Shema* from the book of Deuteronomy, which begins: 'Hear, O Israel: The LORD is our God, the LORD alone. You shall love the LORD your God with all your heart, and with all your soul, and with all your might' (6.4).

- How do we show our love for God?
- Is it by worshipping God or by turning away from other false gods?
- What are the false gods we encounter in our world today – the false gods of materialism, money, power?
- How does honouring the Sabbath show our love for God?
- Is Sabbath more than just a day off, rather a way to set aside time in our busy lives to honour God alone?

Third, we can move from this great commandment of Deuteronomy to talk about how Jesus spoke of the law. There are hundreds of laws in the Old Testament that go beyond these ten. Jesus tried to help people understand their meaning. While some Christians might be apt to say that Jesus liberated us from the law, the Gospels make it clear that he came to help us truly live out the intention of the law. We can talk about how modern Jews still follow many or all of the laws of the Hebrew Scripture and why we as Christians do not. We can talk about how Jesus summarized the meaning of the Commandments – to love the Lord your God with all your heart, mind and soul *and* to love your neighbour as yourself (Matt. 22.37–40).

Finally, we can have a great conversation about how we all fall short of obeying the Ten Commandments. Even though they seem to be straightforward and simple laws, there are many ways that we fail to follow them, ways that we misinterpret them and even ways that we justify disobeying them.

The slippery nature of sin and our struggle to follow these laws was often made clear to me when I watched my confirmation students – so quick, as I said above, to tell me that swearing is a sin – turn into older young people whose conversations and language could at times make my toes curl.

6

The history of Israel

Most Sunday-school materials these days hardly touch on the history of the Kingdom of Israel. Lessons tend to stop at the slaying of Goliath and then pick up again with stories from Daniel. A lot of this history is either too complicated to grasp in a 45-minute Sunday-school lesson or a little too racy or violent for us to feel comfortable teaching it to our children. Or maybe it's just a little too boring for us to find an appropriate craft project or song.

What this means is that not only do students find themselves as teenagers not knowing the details of these major portions of the Old Testament but they have not even been introduced to some of the basic concepts outlined below. These five frame much of the context of the New Testament and are at the foundations of Old Testament theology.

26 The basics

We read of the creation of the Kingdom of Israel in the first book of Samuel, in which God anoints King Saul to rule over God's people, who are in desperate need of strong leadership. For the next several hundred years the Kingdom of Israel will see many greater and even some lesser kings than Saul. There will be wars and bloodshed, espionage and treachery, banquets and debauchery, temples built and rebuilt, exiles and homecomings.

Children should develop a basic awareness of this period of history in the Bible and a general understanding that God's people were led by a king after they settled in the Promised Land.

Planting the seed

I will confess that it is in this area that I feel the least equipped as a parent and a pastor to teach these stories to my son. Yes, I can handle the rest of the items in this chapter pretty well, but the general ascending and descending of kings, battles and other various and sundry details often elude me. I am convinced that the only reason my husband – a biblical scholar himself – can keep everything in the right order is because as a child he had a graphic novel version of the Old Testament.

It is perfectly acceptable to confess to your children that there are things in the Bible you don't know about or don't understand. When these moments arrive, ask your child to be your teacher. My son is always correcting my understanding of Greek mythology, which makes him feel very proud that there are moments when he too can be a teacher. These stories of the Kingdom of Israel are no less interesting – why not ask him to help me learn the Bible as well?

Feeding the soil

One of the things that makes it so hard for me to wrap my head around the history of the Kingdom of Israel is that the Bible does not provide a linear timeline of events or genealogy. In addition, there is significant repetition of stories, not just in the historical books but also when we consider the books of the Prophets – who were advisors or adversaries to many an Israelite king – and Psalms.

In the classroom, children can discover the ways the Old Testament tells these stories in such a layered way. In a lesson on what it meant to be the King of Israel, include a reading of Psalm 72, which describes the characteristics of a king, Jeremiah 21.1–10, on how God spoke to the king through prophets, 2 Kings 25.1–7, on how the king often disobeyed and was punished through defeat at the hands of Israel's enemies, and then Lamentations 5.1–22, on how the people lamented the loss of the kingdom and God's favour during times of exile. As you move through each, take care to point out the different kinds of biblical literature that it takes to tell this epic story – history, prophetic witness, poetry and wisdom.

Watching them grow

An understanding of the Kingdom of Israel can also help students have deeper conversations about why we call Jesus the 'King of the Jews'.

- Why was Jesus so unlike any of these Old Testament kings?
- What does it mean to be prophet and king all wrapped up in one?
- How did Jesus fulfil these responsibilities of the king?

27 Joshua and Judges

There are two things that make the Kingdom of Israel significant. The first is that it represents the land God promised the people when they were slaves in Egypt. But even though God promised them this land, they still had to conquer it before it could become theirs. The book of Joshua tells the stories of those battles and the final settling of the people of Israel in their new home. As long as the Israelites could hold on to this land it was a sign that they were in God's favour.

The second is that initially God told the people that they did not need a king. In times of need, God raised up judges to lead the people in battle and resolve disputes. The people had laws given by God to regulate and organize their society. Yet in the book of Judges we read that time and time again people simply behaved in whatever ways they thought was right. This eventually led them to beg God to give them a king who would rule over them and help them keep the law.

In the next chapter I will talk more about both Ruth (item 38) and Samson (item 40), who lived during the period of the Judges, so below are some ideas for working with children and young people on the book of Joshua.

Planting the seed

According to the book of Joshua, when the Israelites finally conquered and divided the land of Canaan he gathered them together to remind them of all God had done for them and to promise to God that they would leave behind the gods of all of the lands in which they had lived before and worship the Lord alone (Josh. 24).

The most frequently quoted words from that passage are at the end of verse 15 – when Joshua proclaims, 'as for me and my household, we will serve the LORD'. This is a lovely sentiment and looks very nice embroidered on a pillow or hanging above one's mantel. But what does it really mean when we use it in our context today?

Read this final chapter of Joshua with your children and talk together about what it means to make a commitment to God – and what commitments you have made as a family to serve God. Does it mean being part of a church community? Giving to charity? Volunteering your time? Treating people in a certain way? Turning away from the modern 'idols' that can often take God's place in our lives?

Feeding the soil

The most iconic story we teach children from Joshua is the battle at the city of Jericho (Josh. 2 and 6). A major character in this story of conquest is the prostitute Rahab. There are a lot of stories in the Bible that include prostitutes, and as a teacher I would always pause when reading these stories with children. In a lot of instances (such as with Rahab), her identity as a prostitute is somewhat tangential to her role in the story; in others it is absolutely essential.

One can take several approaches in tackling these stories and these women with children in the classroom. First, we can completely gloss over the word 'prostitute' (which is what many children's versions of this story do). Second, we can choose not to teach children these stories until they are older and might be better equipped to understand what a prostitute is. Finally we can be fairly open and honest with children about who she is and what she does. I typically fall in the middle of all of these, depending on the story.

Quite often the Bible ascribes fairly significant acts to prostitutes, who are used as examples of faithfulness in someone who is on the margins of society. It is fine to gloss over the fact that Rahab was a prostitute, but make sure you are able to convey to children in some other way that this was a woman who was on the outside of the Jericho community. She was pressured by the authorities to give up the Israelite spies. She was a woman who in a man's world secured the safety and well-being of all her family. She was remarkable enough to even be included in Matthew's genealogy of Jesus Christ (Matt. 1.5).

Watching them grow

It can be pretty disarming when one fully understands what it meant for the Israelites to inherit the Promised Land. We refer to it as 'the land of milk and honey'. In reality it was a land of bloodshed and devastation. Young people who know these stories can talk about whether it makes us uncomfortable to think about God favouring one army over another or even encouraging the violent removal of people from their land. Other peoples throughout history have claimed God's favour as they have conquered the world and set aside indigenous people. Did they also have God's blessing?

28 David (1 and 2 Samuel)

The call of David from shepherd harpist to giant-killer is one that most children learn either in Sunday school or from a picture Bible. And David's life and adventures don't stop being exciting once he becomes king.

Planting the seed

We tend to focus on teaching children the story of David and Goliath but I believe a much more child-friendly and relatable story is that of David's anointing (1 Sam. 16.1–13).

There is a Cinderella-esque quality to Samuel's review of Jesse's sons. Not finding the one that God had promised would be there, Samuel asks if there might not be one more son he hasn't met yet. As the youngest and smallest, David was not even considered to be in the running, but it is very clear to Samuel that he is the Lord's chosen king. There is a great line in this story where God advises Samuel to be careful and not judge among the sons based on outward appearance – because God doesn't look at things the way humans do.

When David was a child, God chose him for great things. Even though he was small, God saw more to him than his physical appearance. Ask children what gifts they think God has given them to share – kindness, artistic expression, physical strength, compassion, intelligence? We are very good at asking children what they want to do and be when they grow up. But maybe an even more helpful conversation, when we study the story of David, is to ask children what they want to do and be now, today – as a child of God.

Feeding the soil

Instead of focusing only on the stories of David and Goliath, teach children the story of the relationship between David and Saul's son Jonathan (1 Sam. 20). This story serves as a great example of friendship in the Bible, which honestly there is not all that much of. Why not even teach children the story of David's triumphant return to Jerusalem in 2 Samuel 6? This story gives a bigger picture of who David was, what it meant to be king at that time, the role of the Ark of the Covenant for the Kingdom, the relationship between David and his Queen, and even the debates about appropriate ways to worship.

Honestly, the reason we don't typically teach these stories is because they are not easily pulled out of their context in ways that will *make sense to children*. This is exactly the benefit of taking the time and putting in a little more effort not just to tell the stories of David but to teach about the context of ancient Israel.

Watching them grow

We can take the foundation of what older students already know about David as a boy and young man and add in the more complicated elements of his story that made him both a great king and also a sometimes questionable human being. David is a difficult guy to deal with. As young people get older they need to learn how to handle difficult texts like the stories of his relationships with Abigail (1 Sam. 25) and Bathsheba (2 Sam. 11—12), or even that he didn't punish his son Amnon after his assault on his daughter Tamar (2 Sam. 13).

29 The Temple

The Israelites didn't just have a strong connection with the land but with the Temple in Jerusalem, which held the Ark of the Covenant. Typically most students come knowing about the Ark of the Covenant – though I suspect a lot of their imagery for this comes from the Indiana Jones films, as my son's does – but they should also understand that it was kept in the most sacred place in the Temple and that the Israelites believed God dwelt in that place with it.

Planting the seed

Teaching children about the Temple in Jerusalem can be enhanced by using a Bible dictionary – especially an illustrated one – to help children visualize what the Temple would have looked like.[1]

Feeding the soil

We get so caught up in teaching children about David that we sometimes forget to teach about his son and the longest ruling King of

---

[1] One of my favourite children's Bibles is *The Children's Illustrated Bible*, with text by Selina Hastings (London: Dorling Kindersley, 1994, 2000, 2005). With full-colour illustrations and diagrams of the First and Second Temples, children can get a sense of the culture of the Bible and see photo-realistic images of archaeological discoveries as well. It is a meaningful addition to a child's personal Bible resources.

Israel – Solomon. 2 Kings 8 provides a wonderful summary of the history of not just the building of the Temple but of God's promise of the Temple, David's inability to build it and the placement of the Ark of the Covenant within it. Solomon's prayer at the dedication addresses both God's willingness to dwell within the Temple and also the significance of God's protection of the Temple as related to God's favour of Israel as a whole.

If your congregation is in the midst of its own building project and is preparing or has recently dedicated it, take time to read this passage with children. Have children compare Solomon's prayers and petitions with the liturgy that you used in your modern dedication. Even if this is not part of your recent history, most denominations have prayer books that include liturgy for this kind of dedication. Have children use that resource and Solomon's prayer to create their own prayers of dedication for your sanctuary.

Watching them grow

We have such a different world view today as modern people and different ways of talking about *where* God is. It is sometimes hard for students to grasp the idea that these ancient people would have thought that God was located there in the Temple. We tell students all the time that God is everywhere, even in the most un-sacred of places. How do we interpret Scripture based on these differing world views? Talking together about the role of the Temple in the life of the people of Israel will help students understand the significance of the exile, which forms the next item, and even provide a context for what it meant when Jesus talked about the Temple being torn down and rebuilt. For modern students it may sound like an empty threat, but for the Jews who heard it, it was much more significant.

30 The exile

While the circumstances surrounding the Assyrian and Babylonian exiles can seem complicated, it really is enough to give children a sense that God had promised the people of Israel this specific land and then, through foreign attacks and defeats, they were removed from this 'promised' land. This is the moment when the first Temple was destroyed and the people of Israel were forced to rethink their identity and shape a faith separate from their land and their religious centre.

Planting the seed

All children at one time or another have experienced homesickness, and so the songs and laments written during the time of exile can have a cathartic quality about them even for us as modern people. It is rare to find a children's picture Bible that will tell the story of the exile, but you can sit with children and read together Psalm 137 and talk about the feelings the psalmist is expressing – a longing for home, a lack of joy, a hopelessness, desperation. What must it have been like for the Israelites not just to be homesick during the exile but to feel as though God had abandoned them or was maybe even punishing them?

Feeding the soil

We find in the book of Ezekiel one of the most vivid metaphors for exile and restoration among all of the prophets. Ezekiel 37 contains a vision of a valley of dry bones that come back to life and become full of the spirit of God.

Older children around 10–12 years old can slowly be introduced to the ways we use Scripture to inform or give us an understanding of our lives today as individuals, nations and as citizens of the world. Read this story from Ezekiel with them and talk about how the Israelites were exiled from their home and were desperate for hope and homecoming. Then ask them to look together at several newspapers from the past week or month, searching out stories of people who are also desperate for hope and homecoming. Use God's words in verses 11–14 to write a prayer together asking for God's help for these current events.

Watching them grow

What does it means to find restoration through God? Too often we talk with young people about a crisis of faith being all about sin and forgiveness. But they need to be given other ways to understand what it means to be separated from and then restored to a relationship with God and sometimes even the Church. This biblical narrative of exile and homecoming can really resonate with young people if we find the time to make it a part of their religious vocabulary.

7

Cherished passages and characters of the Old Testament

While biblical literacy is one of the main goals that we should set for our children when we are teaching them at home, in the sanctuary or in the classroom, we should also be fostering within them the tools they will need to become theologians.

Theology is the study of God – our relationship to God, the actions and motivations of God and the ways we describe or understand God. The Bible provides rich imagery that forms the basis of most theological language, whether proclaimed from the pulpit or discussed around the dining-room table.

The following are ten passages or stories that can help children have a deeper and broader vocabulary when it comes to describing who God is and how God works in the world. While the books of Genesis and Exodus give us endless examples of the theological concepts of God's covenant with God's people and God's call on the life of the believer (two constant themes throughout the entire Bible), when we dig deeper into the Old Testament we can find even more theological ideas that will serve our children well as they grow in their faith.

31 Psalm 23

The Lord is my shepherd, I shall not want. He makes me lie down in green pastures; he leads me beside still waters; he restores my soul.

Planting the seed

There is something about the language of this psalm that really touches the heart. Maybe it is the connection to moments in our lives when we have turned to it in desperate need of the divine presence and care it describes that makes this specific piece of Scripture so significant for many people. Children don't bring the same associations to their reading of it, and we would hope they don't bring the same kind of experiences that make this description of God's care so meaningful.

But simply sitting with a child to read this psalm together gives you the chance to describe what Scripture means to you. Psalm 23 provides a way to talk about how there are moments in our lives when we go to the Bible simply for comfort. These words remind us of the generations who have come before us who have sought the care and comfort of God in times of distress and pain. We believe that God cares for us in those valleys.

Feeding the soil

I have mixed feelings about asking children to memorize Scripture, but it is crucial to give children and young people the resources and tools they might need to navigate the ups and downs of life. Sometimes a connection to particular pieces of Scripture can be the best tool to employ. Yet when memorization becomes an end in itself and disrupts the classroom experience or a child's ability to participate, it hardly seems worth it.

You can find a happy middle way by integrating key Scripture passages like Psalm 23 into the regular traditions within your class. Create a cycle of important pieces of Scripture – like many in this list – and use them as part of your opening or closing prayers for your time together. Ask children to read them out loud for each other. For a piece like Psalm 23 encourage your leaders and volunteers to share with children what the passage means to them. Ask leaders to suggest what favourite pieces of Scripture – outside what you are regularly covering in your curriculum – they would like to teach the children. You will find that without even realizing it these passages will become part of a child's religious vocabulary.

Watching them grow

I often hear older students talk about wanting the Bible to be something they can turn to for comfort and help when they are in need. I try to share with my students that for me the Psalms provide comfort in knowing that thousands of years before me another person felt the same things. One of my favourites to share with them is Psalm 69, which really helped me find a voice for the struggles I had as a teenager. The simple act of sharing how we as adults have used Scripture in our lives can go a long way towards modelling how the Bible can be a part of students' spiritual lives as well.

32 Proverbs

I have not provided a specific text here for Proverbs, but would instead simply want children to know that there is a book of Proverbs in the Bible and to have a sense of what a proverb sounds like.

Planting the seed

How often do we hear children, young people or even adults describe the Bible as an instruction manual for life? I am not sure where this metaphor is encouraged, but it is not a very apt one considering how instruction manuals are often treated – tossed aside until there is a problem or thrown away because we think we already know how the equipment works.

Even though the Bible doesn't include clear instructions for our modern lives, it does include wisdom. Specifically, books like Proverbs give us snippets of wisdom that can provide fascinating jumping off points for conversations with children. While reading other parts of the Bible one verse at a time often disregards the context in which a verse is rooted, each individual proverb is made to stand alone. Reading one or two short ones with older children can be a great way to talk together about how they understand the world.

Ask an older child to spend some time reading through Proverbs on their own and then to choose a particular proverb they find relatable to talk about with you. We might hope it will be Proverbs 23.22, 'Listen to your father who begot you, and do not despise your mother when she is old.'

Feeding the soil

A fun way to teach children and younger teenagers about the book of Proverbs is by helping them connect these small verses of wisdom to other more modern ways we express 'wisdom' today. For example, here in the USA I have often put proverbs into Chinese-American fortune cookies to help students connect biblical wisdom with a

Confucian style of wisdom. But an even more up-to-date example might be to present individual proverbs as car bumper-stickers, novelty T-shirts or cross-stitched pillows. Assign students their own biblical proverb to work with and to transform into a contemporary medium. Students can share what they think their proverb means and how it might apply to their life today. The goal in this activity is to help them understand the concept of the book of Proverbs rather than expect them to try to consume all of the wisdom – which can sometimes be hard to understand even for adults – contained in the book.

Watching them grow

Older students can have their basic understanding of Proverbs and wisdom opened up even further by reading together from the first three chapters and talking about the personification of wisdom. What might it mean that the Bible talks about wisdom in the feminine? What does it mean when she speaks of being present at the moment of creation? This is just the kind of envelope-pushing stuff that can really open a student's mind to the complexities of the Bible.

33 Ecclesiastes 3.1–8

For everything there is a season, and a time for every matter under heaven: a time to be born, and a time to die; a time to plant, and a time to pluck up what is planted; a time to kill, and a time to heal.

Planting the seed

Even very young children understand that a year is divided into the rhythm of seasons. The writer of Ecclesiastes expands on this metaphor to talk about the seasons of our lives from life to death, prosperity to poverty, hate to love, destruction to building up. This is a larger lesson that we teach our children all the time as their lives are also divided into these rhythms – seasons in school when they succeed and seasons when they struggle, seasons when they seem to be surrounded by friends and seasons when they feel alone and abandoned, seasons when your family is able to do so many of the things they want to do and seasons when activities need to be cut back for whatever reasons. Just as they experience the birth of siblings, they inevitably will also experience the death of older family members.

Reading this beautiful passage from Ecclesiastes can be a way to talk with them about how our lives ebb and flow with both joys and struggles and with hope and despair. God is with us in all of these seasons. The seasons of dark are not the sign of God's absence and the seasons of light are not the sign of God's favour. God has created human beings to live in this world, and each part of that creation and its cycles are part of the life God has made for us. We can hope and pray for the day when life will be free of these cycles but until that day, God moves through them with us.

Feeding the soil

I am always surprised when older students are not familiar with what I think is a pretty familiar and secularized piece of Scripture. Since it is of course based on Ecclesiastes, I have also been known to sing a few verses of the late Pete Seeger's classic song 'Turn! Turn! Turn!' – covered in the mid-1960s to great success by the Byrds – to try to jog their memory, with limited success.

Diane and Leo Dillon have created a beautiful children's book, *To Everything There is a Season*, which imagines these cycles of our lives through different cultures from around the world.[1] Using that book, or using images you can find yourself of people and families from around the world representing these life cycles, read the passage from Ecclesiastes with children. Bringing in modern inter-cultural images especially helps children to think about what daily life and work are like outside their own context. Then ask them to create their own contrasting images to show what they think the difference can look like between life and death, mourning and dancing, silence and speech, embracing and refraining from embrace, and so on, and at what different moments they can occur in our lives.

Watching them grow

The Bible contains many reflections on the human condition and God's part in that condition. Does being a Christian mean there is no suffering or that life is always perfect? How do we as people of faith, people who believe in God, weather the ups and downs of life? We can talk about how not all Scriptures are as relatable as this one;

---

[1] Leo and Diane Dillon, *To Everything There is a Season: Verses from Ecclesiastes* (New York: Blue Sky Press, 1993).

sometimes there are so many culturally specific elements to a story that it is hard to understand how it relates to us today. But then there are Scriptures like this one that could have been written by a modern poet or songwriter.

34 *Isaiah 9.2–7 and 11.1–9*

For a child has been born for us, a son given to us; authority rests upon his shoulders; and he is named Wonderful Counsellor, Mighty God, Everlasting Father, Prince of Peace.

Planting the seed

This passage from Isaiah can be a vehicle to introduce children to the concept of the Messiah. The following is an example of how simple it can be to broach these kinds of biblical themes with them.

I sat with my ten-year-old son, read this passage to him and asked him to whom he thought it referred. Of course he went with the standard answer – Jesus. I asked him why he thought that. If the New Testament is where we find the stories of Jesus, how could there be a passage about Jesus in the Old Testament? I stumped him. So we talked about the role of a prophet like Isaiah to speak to the people on behalf of God. Then we talked about what a Messiah is – someone who is anointed by God to lead the people. I told him that the Old Testament tells us of this Messiah who would come to lead and protect the people of Israel. An easy way to help children connect with this Hebrew concept of a Messiah is to tell them the Greek translation of the same word – Christ.

I reminded him that we often read this passage from Isaiah on Christmas Eve as we are getting ready for the birth of Jesus. He said that some parts of it were not very Christmasy, like the verses about warriors trampling in blood. His own curiosity led us to a whole other conversation about who the people thought the Messiah would be – that he would be a warrior and a great military leader. Then I asked him to describe to me the ways Jesus did not fit that model.

This conversation only took about 15 minutes, snuggling on the couch early on a Sunday morning. It will not be the last time we talk about this theological concept or this particular passage in Isaiah, but it laid the foundation for future conversations.

Feeding the soil

The first time I planned a Christmas Eve lessons and carols service for the families of our congregation, I consulted the traditional liturgy of readings established for this style of service at King's College, Cambridge. Though I had grown up attending an adaptation of this service in my Presbyterian church, I had no idea how many selections were originally assigned from the Old Testament. As a pastor I was never able to integrate as many of them as I might have wanted in our 'family-friendly' service.

In a service like ours maybe the *only* passage read that night from the Old Testament was this one from Isaiah 9 and 11. I know that because it is a little jarring to hear about garments rolled in blood when we are all bathed in candlelight and dressed in our Christmas finest, some people tend to edit out verses 3–5 (the same ones my son referred to as not very Christmasy). But to cut out those verses means we are missing an opportunity – when we actually have children's attention in worship – to allow them to hear the fullness or even the messiness that happens when we read the Old and New Testaments together.

Watching them grow

What was the political and religious role of the prophet? Sometimes the prophet speaks to God. Sometimes he hears a message from God. Sometimes he is called upon to speak that message to a people who are not all that interested in hearing it.

When students are familiar with the two passages above we can also talk further about the Jewish understanding of the Messiah that they reflect and its relationship to our Christian understanding of Jesus.

- Why do we read these passages on Christmas Eve?
- How do they reflect who we understand Jesus Christ to be?

35 Jeremiah 18.1–11

Then the word of the LORD came to me: Can I not do with you,
O house of Israel, just as this potter has done? says the LORD.
Just like the clay in the potter's hand, so are you in my hand,
O house of Israel.

Planting the seed

Children can be very creative in the language and the metaphors they use for God. Once my son told me that God was both a man and a woman – a man during the day and a woman at night. Of course this mirrored his experience of his father and I – his dad being the best at playing during the day and his mother the best at comforting him at night. When we share our names and experiences of God with children, we slowly begin to teach them – sometimes unintention-ally – that there are right and wrong names for God. When children are young they can easily imagine God as a mother, but they hear God referred to as a father enough times that this becomes the more acceptable way for them to imagine God.

Instead of considering some names for God to be right and some to be wrong, we should do two things for our children. First, we should help them understand that no matter what language we use for God none of it will ever fully capture all that God is. Second, we can show them that the Bible gives us a wide variety of names for God. Reading this passage from Jeremiah together jumpstarts that conversation as you help them imagine God as an *artist*, a *craftsman*, a *potter*, shaping the world through his strength and creativity.

Feeding the soil

At church too we have an obligation to introduce children to the wide variety of language used for God, especially in the Old Testa-ment. What does it mean when the psalmist calls God 'our rock and salvation'? Why does God describe himself to Jeremiah as a potter?

This passage from Jeremiah can give children a tactile way to think about a very metaphorical idea. While it may not be feasible to intro-duce children to creating pottery on a wheel (of course if it is, you should), have them create their own clay pots while talking together about how God showed Jeremiah this place and this craftsman to give him a new way of thinking about and describing God's work in the world. What if we understood God as an artist who shapes and moulds the world for a purpose? Pottery is actually a pretty muscly craft – in this text God is not a painter or a musician, but a strong potter who pushes and pulls at the clay and even scraps a project that doesn't work out.

Watching them grow

This passage can be used with older students to talk in more detail about the prophet Jeremiah and to help them understand that there are a host of distinct prophetic voices in the Old Testament. It also introduces the consequences of not honouring the covenant with God – as Israel was supposed to do. How does this passage describe the punishment the people of Israel would have experienced when they were removed from the Promised Land?

36 Jonah

God calls Jonah to preach a word of judgement to the people of Nineveh, and he turns tail and flees across the sea instead. When his boat is troubled by an intense storm, he is thrown overboard and swallowed by a great fish. After Jonah's time of seclusion and prayer, the fish spits him out, and he is once again called by God to preach repentance to the people of Nineveh. He relents, and they repent. The story ends, though, with a part we often forget to teach to children, when Jonah pouts and complains that God is too merciful. God puts Jonah in his place and tells him that the mercy of God is for God's use at his own discretion.

Planting the seed

I have found that the part of Jonah most relatable to children is the ending above, when Jonah is peeved at God for not punishing the people of Nineveh.

Children themselves have this same reaction every time they think justice has not been served to another, punishment has not be given out fairly to a sibling or when the disciplining of a friend falls outside of the black and white ways they have been taught to understand logical consequences. We tell children the same thing God tells Jonah – they have no right to be angry about the giving of mercy to another person.

God is 'merciful, slow to anger, and abounding in steadfast love, and ready to relent from punishing' (Jonah 4.2). Yes there are many instances when God is unrelenting in punishing the people, but there are also stories like Jonah where God's love and mercy are just as strong.

Feeding the soil

Jonah's story is often used with children to reinforce the theological concepts of call and obedience. But Jonah is also a story of prayer, repentance and forgiveness. We move too quickly over the prayer Jonah prays inside the belly of the whale. He is in deep trouble, not just physically but spiritually, and he names his separation from God in his prayer and expresses his trust that God will forgive and deliver him. He prays with thanksgiving for mercy, confident that he will receive – and he does.

Use the prayer of Jonah with older children as you are teaching them how to pray. It has beautiful aquatic language that obviously applies to his current predicament but also describes how any one of us might feel when we are overwhelmed and disconnected from God. As children read this prayer together, ask them if they have ever felt like Jonah describes himself feeling, and remind them that we can still pray Jonah's prayer today whenever we are looking for words to describe these kinds of feelings.

Watching them grow

The story of Jonah allows us to talk about the tradition of folk tales or fables in the Bible. Is there a difference between literal truth and a larger theological truth contained in a story? For the story of Jonah, that truth might be that as humans we are often quick to judge and very quick to assume God's judgement on others. In truth, God's mercy is something we can never fully comprehend, and God's ability to forgive – thank goodness – is much stronger than our own.

37 Daniel

Daniel and his friends are among the Israelite captives taken to live in exile under the Babylonian King Nebuchadnezzar. At one point Daniel is plotted against by some of the king's men and ratted out for his faithful maintenance of daily prayer to God. He is thrown into a den of lions and comes out unharmed.

Planting the seed

When I read this story with my son we talk a lot about how we under-stand miracles in the Bible (more on this in Chapter 10). The story teaches us that the people of the Old Testament believed that God protected them, and that those who were faithful to God would be granted God's protection from those who did not believe. Does this mean that we should jump into the lion's cage at the zoo and trust that our faith in God will protect us? No.

Miracle stories are often pointing us to some other truth or characteristic about God beyond the miracle. Here we can talk with children about how foolishly the king is acting in this story. He doesn't want Daniel to die but he feels obligated to uphold an unjust law. The miracle of Daniel's life is not just about God's power but the witness of one of God's followers living among foolish people who needed a sign of the wisdom of worshipping Daniel's God instead.

Feeding the soil

The story of Daniel and the lion's den epitomizes the ways we carefully edit biblical stories to make them more child-friendly. You might find this story in any collection of children's Bible stories or even in its own picture book. Typically it will end with the den being opened and Daniel emerging to declare God's protection over him and God's ability to close the mouths of the lions against him. Yet when we start reading the actual Bible with children – and read with them through to the real ending of the story – they will quickly notice that it has a much more violent ending than they had previously heard: Daniel's accusers – along with their wives *and* children – are all thrown into the lion's den and, the text tells us, were devoured before they even hit the bottom.

It is really for you to judge when the children in your Sunday-school classes are ready to start making the transition from the child-friendly to the unfiltered versions of the stories. I often have older children sit with the two versions of the story together so they can find the differences. Typically they are pretty understanding that there are some things you might not want to put in a picture book. Showing them that you believe they are ready for the real version of stories from the Bible will encourage them to take the work of reading the Bible seriously, knowing that you have confidence in them. In my experience, waiting too long to help young people make this transition will only lead them to believe that they have been intentionally taught the wrong details to biblical stories.

Watching them grow

Daniel can help us review the time of the exile and what it meant for the people of Israel to be removed from the land they had been given by God. Does that mean that God no longer showed them favour? In these stories we can see that the people came to believe that even in exile, if they were faithful to God, God would be faithful to them. Daniel also provides great fodder for conversations about what it means to have a minority faith. How do we show or live out our faith when the culture in which we exist disagrees with it?

38 Ruth

The story of Ruth is one of the most artfully crafted in Scripture. Ruth is a foreign widow who chooses to care for her Israelite mother-in-law, also recently widowed. Back in Bethlehem she meets a distant relative of her husband who in a generous interpretation of the law marries her and provides for Ruth and her mother-in-law. In addition to the beautiful way the story shows how Old Testament laws might have been interpreted in real-life situations, it also provides a genealogy for the future King David, who is Ruth's great grandson.

Planting the seed

In its simplest interpretation the story of Ruth is about how we are obligated to take care of our family – both nuclear and extended. The laws of the Old Testament were clear about how the community was called to care for the widow but also how they were obligated to take care of family who had fallen on hard times. Ask children to point out to you every time someone in the Bible takes care of another person in their family – Ruth caring for Naomi; Naomi for Ruth; Boaz for both of them.

Feeding the soil

When Ruth goes to Boaz's fields to gather grain she is participating in what was a very traditional way for the poor of the community to receive charity by picking up the leftover grain in the fields. In a conversation with children at church about Ruth, talk about the ways your congregation gives aid or charity to people in your community.

Boaz does something interesting, though: he actually directs his workers not just to be sure to keep Ruth safe but also to allow her to have from the first grain, not just the leftover. Challenge children – and adults – to think about whether we as the Church give from our leftovers or from our own share, sacrificing for the sake of the community. Help them come up with suggestions for how your church might focus your giving in the model of Boaz.

Watching them grow

In this story of Ruth students can learn the practical implications of those endless laws found in books like Leviticus (Lev. 25.35).

- What does it mean to care for other people not just out of obligation but out of what the Hebrew Bible calls *hesed* – most accurately translated as 'loving kindness'?
- What does it mean that the greatest King of Israel is descended from a foreign-born widow?

In a conversation about Ruth we might also take a look at the genealogy of Jesus found at the beginning of the Gospel of Matthew.

- What does it mean for us as Christians to have someone like Ruth in Jesus' family tree?
- Why would the Gospel writer have taken the time to include her?

39 Esther

Esther – a member of the Jewish diaspora living in Persia – is selected to be the new Queen to King Xerxes. In a parallel storyline, one of the King's advisors has it in for the Jews and tricks the king into arranging for their genocide. Once Esther finds out about the plot and is given some pretty forceful encouragement by her uncle, she confronts the King and his advisor and essentially saves her people from annihilation.

Planting the seed

A central theological concept we can talk about alongside Esther is providence. Mordecai challenges Esther to consider what her role is supposed to be in this complex story. What if, he asks, she is in a position of power precisely because it allows her to intervene on behalf of the Jews? Share experiences with children of times you have witnessed God working in your life to put you in a place to help other people or to receive help. While God may not micro-manage our daily lives, there are moments when we need to be open to the call of God and God's ability to put us in the right place at the right time to do good in the world.

Feeding the soil

As we teach Esther we should introduce children to the Jewish holiday of Purim.[2] At a Purim festival the story of Esther is dramatized and participants dress up in costumes and masks. A traditional feast is held and sometimes gifts are exchanged. Investigate how Purim is celebrated by the Jewish communities and incorporate some of these traditions in a wrap-up session on Esther. Encourage children to dress up in costumes and teach them the traditional audience responses that are called out throughout the retelling of the story of Esther.

Watching them grow

Esther provides a great starting point for a deeper discussion of providence and destiny and a call that goes beyond the traditional call stories we find in the rest of the Old Testament. Unlike the patriarchs who came before her, Esther receives no vision and hears no voice of God. All she has are the voices of her family and of her own conscience.

- How will those voices guide her?
- How do they guide us today?
- As young people seriously start to consider who God is calling them to be, how do they hear the voice of their families and communities speaking a word from God to them?

40 Samson (Judges 13—16)

Samson is a Nazirite, which means he neither cuts his hair nor drinks alcohol. For reasons unknown he has developed superhuman strength that allows him to do things like kill lions with his bare hands. Most

---

[2] See Yechiel Eckstein, *How Firm A Foundation: A Gift of Jewish Wisdom for Christians and Jews* (Brewster, MA: Paraclete Press, 1997); also try <www.reformjudaism.org/jewish-holidays/purim>.

of the stories of Samson are tall tales about his feats of strength and his weakness for women. Most prominent is the story of his relationship with Delilah, her betrayal and his destruction of the Philistine Temple and his own death.

Planting the seed

When my son was about seven years old and soon after he had read the story of Samson with me in his children's Bible, we took a trip to the Art Institute of Chicago. Among the collection was a marble sculpture by Christoforo Stati (1556–1619). Done in the Greco-Roman/Italian Renaissance style, Samson is holding open the strong jaw of the lion while their legs intertwine. We stood below the sculpture, and I asked my son if he noticed anything wrong with the piece. It took him about a minute, but eventually he noticed that instead of sporting the long hair of a Nazirite – uncut from the day of his birth – he instead had a decidedly shorter Greek hairstyle. The story of Samson is a strange one, and so one of the simple goals we can set is helping children understand some of the iconic details of these biblical stories.

A stroll through an art gallery or flipping through a book of art together can give multiple opportunities to try to identify biblical stories being conveyed in icons, paintings and sculpture. It is often the tangible details from Scripture that an artist will use to help tell the story, identify the characters and convey a particular interpretation.

Feeding the soil

Most Sunday-school lessons on the story of Samson focus on helping children identify the ways Samson abused his gifts of strength – 'How do we today not appreciate the gifts God has given us?' Or they ask children to reflect on Samson's poor taste in friends (Delilah) – 'How do we allow ourselves to be bullied and tempted by bad "friends"?' There is a place for these kinds of conversations but I am not sure that pulling out the story of Samson is the most effective way to have meaningful and relatable conversations about moral and ethical behaviour with children.

Instead, why not help children come to appreciate the story of Samson, and in fact much of the Old Testament, for what it is – epic ancient literature. Stories like these would have been told and retold in ancient communities until they were eventually compiled together into the book of Judges. Share the story of Samson with children by bringing in a storyteller – or asking a particularly dramatic member of your community – to tell the story as it would originally have been told. When we would do this in my congregation, we took care to dress the storyteller in nondescript 'biblical' clothes from our costume closet, created a story circle on the floor for children, and sometimes my incredibly inventive Christian educator would create a fake campfire with wood and brightly coloured cellophane. There are many biblical values to be taught to children, and a love for the drama of Scripture is one of them.

Watching them grow

The stories of Samson are among some of the most fantastical stories of the 'heroes' of the Bible, but also provide a look at some of the seedier parts of the Old Testament. We often use the phrase 'Bible heroes' to teach children to be more like Abraham or David, but the stories of Samson fit very well into the ancient paradigm of hero as found in other ancient stories, such as those that come from Greece and Rome. Like many of these heroes, Samson has both admirable qualities and character flaws that prove fatal for him in the end. Discussions of Samson can help students reflect on the biblical stories as being part of a larger tradition of ancient stories that take on similar patterns and traditions. Samson, while not necessarily the kind of hero we might admire, is very much a hero in the tradition of Oedipus and Achilles.

8

The Gospels

One of the heftiest assignments I give confirmation students is to read the entire Gospel of Mark and report back to the class what they learned about the life of Jesus, the patterns they noticed or even the things that struck them as odd.

The most memorable reaction to this assignment came several years ago when one of the girls in the class started off the discussion, even before we were ready to start class, by complaining to me: 'Why didn't anyone ever tell me Jesus was so mean?' All I could think of as a response was, 'I am so sorry. I should have told you before.'

When we teach our children about who Jesus is, what he said and what he did, we do so outside the context of reading a standard translation of the Gospels with them. We teach them about Jesus through picture books, nativity sets, children's Bibles, movies, Sunday-school classroom posters and stained-glass windows.

I am not arguing against any of these methods of teaching children about Jesus and how to be followers of Jesus. But as children grow, their understanding and picture of Jesus should grow with them. The Gospels themselves are the best tool to stimulate that kind of evolution of faith.

My precocious student's statement that no one ever told her Jesus was not always warm and fuzzy reflects exactly the kind of epiphany and growth that can happen as students get older. Needless to say, such an epiphany is not possible when a child lacks even a basic knowledge of the Gospels.

The first step in preparing a student to develop an adult understanding of Jesus is helping them understand what a 'gospel' is in the first place.

The word 'gospel' means 'good news', a translation of the Greek word *euangelion* (this is where we get the word 'evangelism', meaning to tell the good news). While 'the gospel' is the good news of Jesus Christ, when we speak of 'a Gospel' we usually mean a book about Jesus' life, ministry and teachings.

It is likely that a child who attends worship or Sunday school regularly has heard of the four Gospels in the Christian Bible. Children should also know about the sequel to the Gospel of Luke, the Acts of the Apostles, which tells the stories of Jesus' followers and the start of the Christian Church.

What children may not be aware of is that each of these books stands alone as a complete story of Jesus' life and ministry. They are not four chapters in one long story of Jesus' life, rather four complete and unique versions of the life of Jesus. This is one of the pitfalls of children's Bibles: they simply pick and choose stories from the Gospels and compile them as though they came from one continuous book.

Below is a brief summary of what makes each Gospel distinctive.

41 Matthew

The Gospel of Matthew is the first book of the New Testament and the second longest of the four Gospels. It is held, together with Mark and Luke, as one of the Synoptic Gospels, meaning that when you look at all three together you can see that they follow the same basic outline of the story of the life, death and resurrection of Jesus of Nazareth.

Biblical authorship is tricky to identify, no matter the book, but the Gospels bring their own unique challenges. Because there is much common material among all four, it is usually held that they were written later in the first century and that they probably used each other as source material. Different scholars hold to different theories about who copied from whom, but most agree that it is highly improbable that the disciple Matthew was the actual author of the Gospel. Instead, his name was likely attributed to the Gospel to give it more authority.

The Gospel of Matthew is sometimes described as the Church's Gospel, and in fact Matthew is the only one that includes the Greek word translated as 'church'. With a focus on discipleship and salvation and the inclusion of more 'teaching materials' – like the Sermon on the Mount – than any of the other Gospels, it was often used as a teaching catechism in the Early Church. Matthew is also distinctive in its extensive references to the Old Testament, quoting it – though sometimes mistakenly – more than any other Gospel.

42 Mark

Mark is typically held to be the earliest of the four Gospels and is far and away the shortest. It is a bare-bones Gospel, including no stories of Jesus' birth and very limited selections of his teaching. Mark moves quickly from one story to the next, stringing the acts of Jesus together in a frantic pace. Tradition held that the Gospel was written by John Mark, a contemporary of Peter and Paul in Rome, but again that authorship is impossible to confirm.

While it may not have all of the bells and whistles of other Gospels, it is an easily tackled reading assignment for older children and young people – a great simple introduction to the full arch of the story of Jesus Christ.

43 Luke

Luke is sometimes referred to as the 'historian' – he opens his Gospel with a dedication to an unknown student, Theophilus ('lover of God'), and claims to be presenting an accurate and orderly account of the life of Jesus of Nazareth. The Gospel of Luke is the longest book of the New Testament.

Luke is distinctive in its prolific inclusion of parables and stories of the birth of John the Baptist and the annunciation to Mary. While Luke draws attention to the Jewishness of Jesus' life, it is also highlights the inclusion of the Gentile – non-Jewish – world in the saving work of Jesus Christ. Luke is unique as a Gospel in that it is the first part of a two-part narrative completed in the Acts of the Apostles (see below).

44 John

The Gospel of John stands alone in both its content and its provenance. It does not follow the same outline of events as the other three Gospels and contains a significant amount of material unique to itself. John may have been the latest of the four Gospels to be written, and again, while its authorship was traditionally attributed to the disciple John, most scholars point to a much later writer. The author never claims to be the disciple John, but within the story there are frequent references to a 'beloved disciple', who is considered to be John.

John is distinctive in its Christology. While other Gospels might focus on what Jesus did and said, John points to who Jesus is. The Gospel begins with the preface describing Jesus as the Word of God present with God from the beginning. It is from John that we have received the language of Jesus as the Good Shepherd, the Bread of Life, the True Vine and so on.

45 The Acts of the Apostles

Finally we have the second part to Luke's Gospel, which chronicles the lives and ministry of the first apostles after Jesus' resurrection. This book includes stories of Paul's conversion, the ways the first Christians shaped community, the struggles they had with both Jewish and Roman authorities and the internal conflicts they endured as they began to evangelize and grow outside the historically Jewish community.

A helpful detail to keep in mind is the difference between a disciple and an apostle, because we sometimes use them interchangeably. A disciple is a student, one who is subject to the discipline of a teacher. An apostle is literally 'one who is sent'. While we might use 'disciple' to describe anyone who has become a follower of Jesus Christ and his teachings, the apostles were specifically those sent out into the world to spread the teachings of Jesus.

Planting the seed

The best and simplest way to teach older children about the diversity among the Gospels – as with teaching children anything from the Bible – is to sit down together with a Bible and read stories from the Gospels together. Help them learn to look up passages from the Gospels and Acts. Teach them their order in the New Testament. It is as simple as that.

In the rest of this book you will find stories and passages from all four Gospels and Acts. As you read each of them together with your child, make sure that you point out which Gospel each story comes from. Take time to read any introductory material at the start of each biblical book, which will help children recognize the themes of that Gospel.

Feeding the soil

As we teach children the stories of the Gospels, we often select which Gospel version of the story best fits both the age to which we are teaching and the activities we have planned. But what would happen if every time we taught children a story from the Gospels we made a point to have them read every version of the story that we have? It wouldn't really take up that much extra class time, and it would be a great way to spark conversation about any differences they notice. A detail that might be overlooked if they only read one version could all suddenly become significant when they feel its absence in another.

Through this very simple and consistent practice, we help them recognize and appreciate the diverse voices within the Bible.

It will also mean that when they learn a story that is only found in one of the four Gospels, they will get a sense of the colour and voice of that particular book. Without even realizing it, they will come to appreciate the parables of Luke, the beautiful statements of Jesus' divinity in John, the connection to the Old Testament in Matthew, and that, yes, sometimes, in Mark, Jesus seems to be in a big hurry, which can be a little offputting.

Watching them grow

If older students have a foundation of this kind of basic knowledge of the Gospels, then we can spend time talking about the ways Jesus is actually a little more edgy and a little less cuddly than their Sunday-school teachers may have led them to believe.

In addition, we wrestle with the following questions:

- Who wrote the Gospels and how were they used by the first Christian churches?
- Why do they seem so similar and yet so different?
- How does each Gospel portray Jesus?
  - Is he impatient?
  - Is he a storyteller?
  - Is he a political activist?
  - Is he a keeper of wisdom?

- Why do some Gospels have stories of Jesus' birth while others start at the beginning of his ministry?
- Why don't the Gospels tell more stories – or any stories – of Jesus as a child or as a teenager?
- How and why were these four Gospels chosen to be included in the Bible while others were rejected?

9

Moments and miracles in the life of Jesus

————•◦•————

Thirty-five items on this list deal directly with the life and ministry of Jesus Christ. Each one of these stories in the next two chapters allows us to participate in the centuries-old search to understand the fullness of who this man Jesus of Nazareth was, is and will be:

- son of Mary and Joseph
- Son of God
- promised Messiah
- prophet
- liberator
- king of the Jews
- rabbi and teacher
- beloved of God
- miracle worker
- fully human yet without sin.

For each follower of Christ, each of these names, these identities and these traditions will have significance throughout a lifetime of faith. As students grow into their faith and publicly declare themselves to be one of his followers, we serve them best by giving them, even from a young age, the fullest possible picture of Jesus Christ.

The first five stories, in particular, shape the rhythm of our worship from Advent all the way up to Holy Week and are essential starting points for conversations about who Jesus was and what that means for us as his followers.

The second five stories focus on a selection of the miracles Jesus performed during his earthly ministry. While understanding Jesus as a miracle worker, as students get older they can understand how he used miracles not just to illustrate his divinity but to show the world as God intended it to be.

46 The stories of Jesus' birth (Matthew 1—2; Luke 1—2)

These birth narratives come entirely from the Gospels of Matthew and Luke. In Matthew we read of the angel appearing to Joseph; the visit of the magi to the holy family in Bethlehem; the warning of Joseph in a dream to flee from Israel with his newborn child; the slaughter of the innocents by King Herod; and finally the sojourn of the holy family in Egypt.

Luke gives us the announcement of the birth of John the Baptist to Elizabeth and Zechariah; the visit of an angel to Mary and Mary's response in faith; the companionship of Mary and Elizabeth; the journey of Mary and Joseph to Bethlehem; the birth of Jesus in a stable; and finally the announcement of the birth to shepherds in the fields and their adoration of the baby.

Planting the seed

We own several nativity sets as a family. When my son was young I always tried to make sure that he helped us in setting them up during Advent. (See my note on item 81 about waiting to set out baby Jesus until Christmas day). One set that we received as a wedding present is made of baked and painted salt dough from Peru. It is brightly coloured and gives the appearance of being very child-friendly, and certainly was very attractive to a five year old. One drop, though, and pieces easily broke. But they were also easily glued back together. After being frustrated at the first few repairs, I decided that if my son wanted to play with it, I was willing to keep fixing it. His engagement was more valuable than the nativity set.

That being said, there are plenty of nativity sets made these days specifically for children to play with, and since these are really the only biblical stories that we regularly create a tableau of in our homes and churches, we shouldn't miss the opportunity to allow children to play imaginatively with them, either with us or on their own.

Feeding the soil

Speaking of nativity sets, one of my favourite interactive displays we created for children at church involved gathering up every old or new nativity set that we had for use in classrooms from around the church and sorting them by 'character'. Children visited different stations for each character in the birth stories. This meant having an angel station, a Mary station, a Joseph station, shepherds, wise men and so on. At each station they could touch the pieces, notice the differences from different styles of nativities and then read – or have read to them – a short reflection on each member of the story.

Watching them grow

Because these 'Christmas' stories are so familiar to students, they are easier for them to compare and contrast than most other biblical stories. Students can start to ask these kinds of questions:

- Is one version right and one wrong?
- Is it right to mesh the two together as we do every Christmas Eve and in many nativity scenes?
- Can these stories give us insight into the larger message of each respective Gospel?
- How do these stories serve as an example of the ways the writers of the New Testament included images and traditions from the Old Testament?

47 Jesus lost in the Temple (Luke 2.41–52)

Jesus is 12 years old and travelling with his parents and their larger community to Jerusalem for the Passover celebrations. On the return trip, Mary and Joseph realize that Jesus is not among their caravan and return to the city to find him. After searching for three days, they find him in the Temple in deep theological and scriptural conversation with the teachers there. My favourite thing about this story is the context in which it was set – the regular participation of a seemingly normal first-century Jewish family in the annual pilgrimage to Jerusalem for the Passover.

Planting the seed

I have always been fascinated by the fact that it took an entire day for Jesus' parents to realize he was missing. What a contrast with the hyper-vigilant parenting most of us do today. This story always makes me consider the extent to which we trust our children and give them grace and freedom when they are participating as part of the community of faith. Do we let them go off with their friends at church, trusting they will not get themselves in too much trouble? Is our church community a place where children are kept safe even when parents are not around?

Reading this story early with children can help them start to think about how they fit in the community of faith. How do they respect and trust the other adults who are part of their church? Talk with them about how you want them to handle challenges and conflicts that come up when they are at church and you are not around.

Feeding the soil

Most children can fully relate to the anxiety of being lost or separated from their parents. The reactions, though, are flipped in this story: Jesus is calm and the parents are anxious and frustrated.

Find several artistic interpretations of the story – which can be as easy as searching the web for images of 'Jesus lost in the Temple' – and look at them with children. After reading the story, have them describe the emotions they see on the faces of Mary and Joseph; the way Jesus is presenting himself at the Temple; the way the rabbis and priests are listening to and learning from him. Then have them create their own interpretation of the story, taking into account how they will use faces and body language to convey the emotions *they* think each character is feeling in the story.

Watching them grow

This story can provide some great conversation points to explore what it means that Jesus was a practising Jew. Somehow that concept often eludes students. It was important to show that Jesus was a part of the Jewish community and that his ministry should be understood in that context. Additionally, this story is a great way to talk about Jesus' divinity.

- Did Jesus know that he was the Son of God when he was a child?
- Did he already understand his calling to ministry?
- Was he born understanding the Scriptures?

48 Jesus' baptism (Matthew 3; Mark 1.9–13; Luke 3)

Jesus inaugurates his ministry by coming to the place where John the Baptist is preaching along the Jordan River and asking for baptism himself. In some accounts John refuses, saying that it should be Jesus who baptizes him. Upon Jesus' baptism a voice proclaims Jesus the beloved of God, and the Holy Spirit comes upon or appears to come upon him like a dove.

Planting the seed

When we read children's versions of Bible stories or even some adult translations, language is often simplified. It is not unusual for the voice from heaven that speaks at Jesus' baptism to simply say, 'This is my son, whom I love.' The Greek here, though, in all three Gospels, uses a word that is most accurately translated as 'beloved'. This language may seem antiquated, but in its beauty it represents Jesus' identity as the beloved of God. Talk with your children about what it means to be 'beloved'. Whose beloved are they – yours, God's, their grandparents', for example? Talk about the relationship between Jesus and God as parent and child – *lover and beloved*.

Feeding the soil

It is fun to help children imagine this wild man who lived in the desert, ate wild honey and locusts and preached to crowds while standing knee-deep in the Jordan river. It is a little scary, but certainly memorable. We sometimes even treat children to insect-shaped candies/sweets and a variety of honeys to sample to get into the spirit of John the Baptist. Older children, though, should be introduced to the fact that those who saw or even just heard of John in the first century would have been reminded of the prophet Elijah. Don't just stop at reading the stories of John's preaching at the beginning of the Gospels, but also include Mark 6.14–29, which tells of the death of John and the questions about his relationship to Jesus and to Elijah. Also try reading with them from the prophet Malachi, chapters 4 and 5, which speak of the coming of the Messiah and the coming of Elijah to prepare the way.

Watching them grow

- How does this story of Jesus' own baptism shape our theology of baptism today?
- If baptism is about being washed of our sins, why would Jesus need to be baptized?
- How does the act of baptism mark us as beloved children of God?
- What role does the Holy Spirit play in our baptism?
- Where is the power in baptism?
  - Is it in the community?
  - Is it in the promises made?
  - Is it in the actions of the pastor or priest who 'celebrates' it?
  - Is it in the work of the Holy Spirit?

49 The temptation in the wilderness (Matthew 4.1–11; Mark 1.12–13; Luke 4.1–13)

Jesus is led by the spirit into the wilderness so that the devil might tempt him. On three occasions the devil tries to tempt Jesus into abusing his power as the Son of God – tempting him to perform miracles, to test the power of God and to abandon God and worship him instead. Jesus resists each time and leaves the wilderness to begin his teaching and itineration.

Planting the seed

For most of these stories, simply sitting together with children and reading the Bible regularly will be enough to plant the seed of biblical literacy and theological sensibilities. Sometimes, though, they do provide the chance to talk with children about their own lives and experiences. It might be hard for children to understand fully the temptations and responses that go on between the devil and Jesus in this story. Were these 'dares' really all that bad? On one level you can start talking with them about Jesus' desire always to trust and respect God. Doing any one of these things would be disrespectful or show that he didn't need God. But you can also talk with children more specifically about the temptations they face – to lie, to cheat, to be mean. How do they resist these temptations?

Feeding the soil

Both Jesus and the devil are quoting from the Old Testament. Read the full story and ask children how they can tell that both of the characters are quoting verses from somewhere else. They might recognize key markers in the passage like the phrase 'it is written', or they might be looking at a version that indents these quotes to show that they are separate from the story. Then give them the direct citations to look up for themselves (Deut. 8.3; Ps. 9; Exod. 17.12; Deut. 6.13). Do they notice any differences in the language between the Old Testament and how it is quoted in the New Testament? Remind children that during Jesus' life the only Scriptures were the books we now call the Old Testament. The New Testament would not have been written until after Jesus' death.

Watching them grow

This story of Jesus' temptation is how we begin the season of Lent – a season of reflection on our human condition, our tendency towards sin and our need for redemption and connection with God through Christ.

- What does it mean to be fully human and fully divine?
- What does it mean that Jesus lived a sinless life?
- Was he really tempted in the desert?
- Could he really have been persuaded by the devil?
- How does Jesus' human life connect us to him as human beings ourselves?
- As the one who forgives us our sins, what does it mean that Jesus was tempted as we are?
- What does it mean that we have a God who chose to take on our weaknesses?

50 The transfiguration (Matthew 17.1–13; Mark 9.2–13; Luke 9.28–36)

Jesus takes three of his disciples up a mountain with him to pray: Peter, John and James. In the course of his praying he is transformed – or transfigured – before their eyes. His face and clothing begin to glow white. Next to him appears both the prophet Elijah – who was prophesied to return immediately preceding the Messiah – and Moses.

Planting the seed

In many of the suggestions I give for community and classroom activities, I encourage teachers to have children look up corresponding or related passages in other parts of the Bible to help them have a broader understanding of the biblical story. But this is also something easily done at home. With a strange story like Jesus' transfiguration, it may help children to read the story of Moses on the mountain in the book of Exodus. After reading the story of the transfiguration, tell your child that this strange thing that happened to Jesus had happened to another man in the Bible before, in fact one of the same men who met Jesus on the mountain that day – Moses. Then read together Exodus 34.29–35. Talk with children about why they think Moses', and Jesus', face was shining like that. What do they think it would feel like to talk directly to God?

Feeding the soil

This story rarely finds its way into the regular rotations of children's Sunday-school materials, but for any community that uses the Revised Common Lectionary it is regularly included in worship once a year on the Sunday just before Ash Wednesday – or rather, the last Sunday of Epiphany. This story pairs so perfectly with the story of Jesus' baptism that they are the bookends shaping the season of Epiphany. Use this story of Jesus' transfiguration to help students think even more deeply about what is happening in Jesus' baptism. How many connections can they find? What are the differences?

Watching them grow

As Christians we tend to prioritize mountain-top experiences in our personal journeys of faith.

- What if we never have a mountain-top experience?
- What if the heavens never open to give us a vision of God?
- How do we root our belief and faith in ancient stories when even the people in the stories themselves struggle to understand?
- When we do have a mountain-top experience, how do we handle the walk back down the mountain or a remaining life on the plains or even in the valleys?

51 The feeding of the 5,000 (Matthew 14.13–21; Mark 6.30–44; Luke 9.10–17; John 6.1–15)

Jesus has been teaching at length to a large crowd of people, and when the time has come for them to eat there is not enough food. The disciples urge Jesus to send the people to go and find food on their own. Jesus urges the disciples to take the meagre supplies they have and make them stretch to feed the masses.

Planting the seed

John's version of this miracle is a nice one to use to introduce children to the story. In the other versions the disciples seem to gather up the little bit of food they can find from among their own supplies. In John it is a young boy who brings his own food and shares it with Jesus and the crowd. Talk with children about generosity. How does the good that we do in the world grow beyond our small gifts and gestures? While we may not be able to give a lot, we can never know how God will use a simple act of kindness to affect others greatly.

Feeding the soil

When teaching children about Communion, expand the stories they read together to include feeding stories like this miracle and ask them to note the similarities in how Jesus 'presides' over the meal. How does this miracle illustrate the vision that we have for the heavenly banquet? Help them find other 'feeding' stories in the Old and New Testaments.

Watching them grow

Some argue that the miracle in this story is not that food was created out of thin air but that others, seeing the generosity of the disciples, were inspired to pull out and share what they had brought. Instead of the perception of scarcity, the crowd was astonished by the reality of abundance. It is a lovely way to try to explain away a miracle, and so we should *not* teach this interpretation as fact, because students will cling to it a little too easily. Miracles are supposed to make us uncomfortable, and you shouldn't ease that burden too quickly. Instead, you can pull from this creative interpretation the valuable concepts of scarcity and abundance and talk about what it means that Jesus tells us that we are to live abundantly.

52 Walking on water (Matthew 14.22–33; Mark 6.45–52; John 6.15–21)

The disciples have been sent away from Jesus to spend the night on their fishing boat while Jesus prays alone. Jesus comes out to them on the boat, walking on the surface of the water. In some Gospel versions they mistake him for a ghost; then – only in Matthew – Peter asks Jesus to call him out so that he too can walk on the water. When Peter inevitably sinks, Jesus chides him, 'You of little faith'.

Planting the seed

I always struggle with this miracle, since it sometimes just feels like Jesus is needlessly showing off. Yet this image and idea of Jesus walking on water is one of the most common ways we describe his miraculous abilities. So though I might be inclined *not* to make time to sit down and read this story with my son, it is still an essential image of Jesus of which he should be aware. When we read stories like this together, it is not about sharing the 'correct' interpretation of the text that children should come to believe. It is about talking together about something outside of all of our experiences, asking children what they think about the story and being prepared, when they ask for our opinion, to say, 'I don't know. I'm 39 years old and still trying to figure it out myself.'

Feeding the soil

There are not many opportunities to incorporate science experiments in our Sunday-school materials, so when we have the chance we should take advantage of it. For some children this may be the thing that finally sparks their imagination when it comes to reading the Bible. Find simple experiments to teach children about buoyancy and water tension. You can find two very good ones online in various versions – search 'Does a peeled orange sink?' and 'Water tension and pepper'. After getting thoroughly wet, read this story together and talk about how one of the characteristics of miracles is that God acts outside of the laws of science as we understand them.

Watching them grow

Obviously there are many expressions in the English language that come directly from the Bible, and their meaning is coloured by the stories from which they are taken. A common saying pulled from this story is Jesus' comment to Peter – 'O ye of little faith'. What did Jesus mean by this?

- Did he mean that if only Peter were more faithful, he too would have been able to walk on water?
- Did he mean that if Peter had more faith, Jesus would have been able to help him walk on water?
- Did he just mean – as we tell all children when they are learning to swim – that they just need to trust themselves and they will float in the water and not drown?

53 The raising of Lazarus (John 11.1–45)

In John's Gospel Jesus has a particularly close relationship with Mary, Martha and their brother Lazarus. This is why it seems strange when, upon hearing of Lazarus' ill health, Jesus waits to go to him until after he has died. It does allow for a wonderful scene between Jesus and the sisters, and the occasion for what many students have come to know as the shortest verse in all of Scripture – 'Jesus wept'. Jesus goes to the tomb, asks for the stone to be removed and calls Lazarus to wake up and come out – which he obediently does.

Planting the seed

One thing that is interesting to highlight for children is the relationship Jesus has with Lazarus and his sisters. When he weeps with Mary and the other mourners it is not because he is grieving the loss of his friend, since he knows that he will soon be raised. He weeps out of compassion and sympathy for their grief. You can jump from that to talk about how God loves and has sympathy for us in our problems. This is why God came to earth in Jesus Christ – to show us how he shares in our suffering just as Jesus weeps with Mary.

Feeding the soil

While sometimes dramatizing a Bible story reinforces details, another even simpler technique is to convert the story into a reader's theatre script. This basically means dividing the story into the different voices and creating a voice for multiple narrators – and for this one even a collective chorus of the gathered crowds or the voices of the disciples together. Assign the children each a character to read and ask them to use their voices to convey the emotions and reactions they think their characters would express. With all of the crowd reactions, this particular story can take on the flavour of a Greek drama.

Watching them grow

- Does Jesus really let Lazarus die just so he can perform this miracle of resurrection?
- Does Jesus sometimes do things just for show – just for the spectacle?
- Does God let bad things happen to us today just so we can later experience God's grace?
- Why does Jesus weep if he knows Lazarus will be resurrected?
- Is God affected by our pain as Jesus was affected by the sadness of Mary and Martha?
- Does God weep with us at our losses?

54 Water into wine (John 2.1–11)

Jesus, his disciples and his mother are in attendance at a local wedding. When the wine is just about to run out, Mary comes to Jesus to compel him to solve the problem. Jesus' response to his mother is often read as being a little rude, but he complies and turns several containers of water into superior wine.

Planting the seed

Reading this story with children is mostly about increasing their biblical literacy. When I sat to read it with my son recently, I asked him if he had ever read the story before. He had not, though he did know that Jesus turned water into wine. Often, reading the Bible with children is also about increasing their contextual understanding of Jesus. What was interesting in this particular moment of reading was when my son picked up on the last verse, which mentions that Jesus left Cana for Capernaum in the company of his mother, brothers and disciples. 'I didn't know Jesus had brothers?!' This turned then into a short but important conversation about how we are not exactly sure what Jesus' family looked like, but that there are places where his siblings are mentioned. In this brief conversation my son was able to gain a slightly more complicated idea about who Jesus of Nazareth was.

Feeding the soil

Throughout his ministry Jesus uses readily available objects to teach and to inspire. A favourite line of mine from my denomination's Directory for Worship reminds us of this and the way Jesus sanctified the ordinary.

> In his ministry, he used common things like nets, fish, baskets, jars, ointment, clay, towel and basin, water, bread, and wine. Working in and through these material things, he blessed and healed people, reconciled and bound them into community, and exhibited the grace, power, and presence of the Kingdom of God.[1]

Create a lesson for children that includes all of these kinds of items and read stories like this from John to help them imagine how Jesus used common items like water and wine to spark the imagination of his followers.

Watching them grow

John is all about signs and miracles – including the raising of Lazarus mentioned above. It both shows students that each Gospel has its own colour and theological perspective on the life and ministry of Jesus and helps them talk about what kinds of signs we recognize in our world today.

- Are there signs that Christ is coming again?
- Are there signs that God is at work in the world?
- Are there signs that the Holy Spirit is still among us today?
- Who gets to recognize these signs and who interprets them?

55 The healing of the paralytic (Matthew 9.2–8; Mark 2.1–12; Luke 5.17–26)

Often, healing stories are just about Jesus and the one who is healed. But here a group of men take action to secure healing for their friend by extraordinary means. Jesus is teaching in a home that is packed full, and yet these men know that Jesus is the only hope their paralyzed friend has for healing. They take him up – prone on his bed – to the roof of the house, pull open a hole in the tiles, and lower him down

---

[1] Directory for Worship, Presbyterian Church (USA), W-1.3032.

to Jesus. Jesus witnesses the faith of the friends, and upon the forgiveness of his sins the man is healed.

Planting the seed

What does it mean to be an advocate for someone in need? These men who put their friend's needs ahead of their own knew that Jesus could help him, and so they worked together to find a way to get him that help. Sometimes we advocate for others in the same way – standing up for each other, helping someone get what they need, taking care of their physical needs. But sometimes we also advocate for them through prayer, bringing their concerns to God. Older children can understand that in fact the act of the friends carrying this man to Jesus was actually an act of prayer as they brought their concerns to the Son of God – God incarnate.

Feeding the soil

Most likely part of your worship includes offering prayers of intercession for the world and your community. Help children create their own intercessory prayer modelled after the type they would have already heard in worship – whether free-form or responsive. Who do they think needs to be advocated for in the world? In your community? In their family? Among their own friends? If possible, use the prayer they create here in a subsequent worship service in your church, making sure to point out that it came from a lesson on the story of the healing of the paralytic, and reminding children and adults alike that just as Christ advocates for us with God, we are called to intercede for each other and the world with Christ.

Watching them grow

This story opens up a lot of questions about how faith, prayer and healing all work together in our lives today. We pray for our friends and family when they are sick and dying. We talk about the power of prayer and the support we give each other in prayer. Yet unlike the faith of these men, which compels Jesus to offer healing, our faith and our prayer is sometimes not enough. This can lead to questions about how we experience Jesus today. We thank God when someone gets better; should we curse God when they don't? Does the risen Christ still work miracles of healing?

10

Cherished stories of the New Testament

Ask any young person what Jesus Christ did and probably their first answer will be that he died for our sins. This is the essential biblical and theological statement that they hear over and over again. The cross is the central focus of our worship and devotion. Jesus' death is one of the most identifiable things about his life.

Yet as previous and later chapters illustrate, Jesus' life was full of significant acts and teachings, both before and after his death. It is through the lens of his life that we understand his death. It is through the experience of his resurrection that we can understand the real power and love of God who will not leave us abandoned.

In this chapter are included some of the most cherished stories of the Gospels. These are stories that we use to understand Jesus' call on our lives, just as he called the disciples, Zacchaeus or even the Samaritan woman. They are also the stories that remind us of our calling to be different from the rest of the world in how we treat one another and how we worship God, as we read of in the Sermon on the Mount or even in Jesus' casting out the money changers from the Temple. And as we read the stories of his final days, his death and resurrection, we are reminded of his call to walk the way of the cross with him so that we too might have life and have it abundantly.

We can begin this walk with Christ from an early age. We can walk it hand in hand with our children, teaching them the way, telling them the stories, singing the songs of our faith together. As they get older our children will choose whether or not to continue this walk on their own. That choice should not be taken lightly. No matter how many times they have been shown the way, it is still a serious decision. But if they have walked it with us before, we can be sure that it will be a genuine and informed decision.

56 The call of the disciples (Matthew 4.18–22; Mark 1.16–20; Luke 5.1–11)

Jesus' disciples are depicted in the Gospels as sort of a rag-tag group of men who came to him from a variety of social locations and positions in the community. Despite their diversity, we still tend to think of them primarily as a group of fishermen – probably because of this story of Jesus calling Simon, Andrew, James and John to leave their nets behind so that he might make them fishers of men.

Planting the seed

The New Testament doesn't have as many stories about family relationships as the Old Testament, but these two pairs of fishing brothers provide fodder for some good conversations about what it means to share faith within a family. James and John had their own sibling rivalry issues but generally speaking these brothers decided to walk this path of discipleship together. This can lead to conversations about how our faith is also reflected in the way we treat people even within our own family. Does faith – or faithful living – stop at the door to your home, in the family room, in the backyard?

Feeding the soil

One of the ways I always try to illustrate this story to children is to talk with them about fishing in the first century. (In my particular context, commercial fishing is not the first image that comes to their minds.) Read through a variety of stories that show the disciples fishing, such as this call story and a post-resurrection story like John 21.1–14, and talk together about how they used nets to catch fish instead of a fishing pole. I like to bring a fishing net to show them and cast it around or on top of them. What did Jesus mean when he said that he would teach them to fish for people – or in the words of the King James Version, to be 'fishers of men'? We would talk together about the grace that comes with a net instead of a pole. In his ministry Jesus came to teach and to love many people – *he cast a wide net*. He didn't pick and choose, but opened his arms wide to welcome any who would follow him.

Watching them grow

This story serves as the foundation for a conversation about our own calls both to be a follower of Jesus Christ and to other service in the Church, either ordained or as a lay person.

- Does Jesus only call the perfect and the equipped?
- How does God use the unique gifts we are each given to serve the Church and the world?
- What does it mean to leave something behind, as the fishermen left their nets behind, in order to answer Christ's call?

57 The Sermon on the Mount (Matthew 5.1—7.29)

These three chapters in the Gospel of Matthew contain a unified collection of Jesus' major teachings. Chances are, if you think you know something Jesus said or taught, it came from the Sermon on the Mount. Here is where we get our Christian understanding of forgiveness, of prayer and of reconciliation. The sermon also contains a variety of examples of how Jesus interpreted the laws of the Old Testament.

Planting the seed

Use these three chapters in Matthew as a source for daily devotions as a family. They can easily be broken into very short sayings and teachings. Most translations will actually insert headings for the different topics, which provide natural starting and stopping points. For each, or on each day, talk together about what you think Jesus is trying to say and how you think you might be able to follow these instructions together.

Feeding the soil

A creative way to introduce younger teenagers aged around 12 to 14 to the Sermon on the Mount is by making prayer stations that carry them through a guided reading of these three chapters from Matthew. Using a variety of artistic interpretations of Jesus – paintings, drawings and so on – I divide the sermon into about 15 chunks and create separate stations for each one. Students each start at a different station and are given about five minutes to read the passage and reflect on the piece of art assigned to it. At the ringing of a bell they move to the next and continue through this process until they have visited all the stations. At the end I ask them to go and find the piece of art they were most affected by and share with the group what they saw in the art and in what they read from Matthew.

Watching them grow

One who chooses to walk this path of Christian faith needs to know that it is not an easy journey. We are expected to love our enemies, resolve disputes with our friends quickly, refrain from judging others, let our light shine brightly in the world.

- How do we do all of these things?
- Are we supposed to do all of these things?
- Can you call yourself a Christian and choose to ignore some of them?
- To whom are we accountable as Christians for following these laws?
  - God?
  - Each other?

58 The woman at the well (John 4.4–42)

Jesus travels into Samaria, a place usually avoided by devoted Jews. He stops at a public well and speaks there with a woman who has come to draw water. What follows is the longest conversation Jesus has with any one person in any of the four Gospels. He and the Samaritan woman debate theology and in particular the promised coming of the Messiah. Jesus reveals himself to her as that Messiah, and she in turn evangelizes in her local village, bringing her community to come and meet Jesus for themselves.

Planting the seed

One of my greatest frustrations is the reality that many of these prominent stories of women in the Gospels are not included in children's picture Bibles. Even though the visual images from this story could be beautifully illustrated for children, the traditional interpretation – that the woman was ostracized from her community because of sexual immorality – makes it seem like this is not a story for children.

But it actually is a perfectly fine story to read together with children. Any implications of her past are vague enough not to have an impact on a child's understanding of the story. The very best part is that this unnamed woman has a significant give and take with Jesus on biblical, theological and possibly even sacramental issues.

Feeding the soil

The New Testament also lends itself to learning more about the geography of the Holy Land. Just as you can find maps that illustrate the journeys of Abraham and Sarah or even the Exodus, there are all kinds of maps that can help children understand the extensive travelling Jesus did during his three years of active ministry. Look together at a map to understand better where Samaria was and even talk about why Jews went out of their way to avoid it. Have children locate iconic cities and regions from the Gospels – Nazareth, Bethlehem, Jerusalem, Jericho, Galilee, Judea.

Watching them grow

Once students have a larger understanding of the overarching story of the Gospels, we can talk about how women are or are not represented in them.

- Why are so many of them unnamed?
- How does Jesus treat women compared to how women were treated by others in that ancient culture?
- What does it mean that Jesus seems to know all about this woman?
- In our relationship with Jesus, do we feel like Jesus 'knows' us as well?
- How does the writer use the image of water in this story?
- How do these images of water influence the way we understand our baptism?
- What does it mean that the water of baptism is 'living' water?

59 Zacchaeus the tax collector (Luke 19.1–10)

Jesus comes to the town of Jericho and, as always, is mobbed by those who want to hear him teach. Zacchaeus, a tax collector, decides to climb a tree to get a better view. Jesus sees him in the tree, calls him by name and tells him to come down so that he can give dinner to

Jesus and his friends. The crowd is shocked that Jesus would go to the home of a tax collector. Why?

Planting the seed

'Zacchaeus was a very little man, a very little man was he.' Unfortunately this popular song was how generations of children learned the story of this tiny outsider, giving no indication of the real reason why it was so shocking that Jesus would call him by name and invite himself to Zacchaeus' house for dinner. When we read a story like this at home with children, we should push past the Sunday-school version of the story to really talk with children about why people were so shocked at Jesus' behaviour. Probably children won't be able to understand the cultural issues surrounding tax collecting in the first century, but they will understand that there are people who are considered 'unscrupulous' or 'bad' in this world. While we believe that all people sin and make mistakes, there are some sins we have a hard time believing God can forgive. Talk with children about God's love – Jesus' love – being not just for the good people in this world but for those *we* might label as undeserving.

Feeding the soil

One of the criticisms Jesus is subjected to in his life is that *he eats with tax collectors and sinners*. This ubiquitous phrase begs the question of how often he actually did that, or rather of how many stories we have of Jesus doing it. Talk to children about Jesus' practice of sharing meals with people who were considered unclean or bad. Instead of just giving them a list of additional stories to look up to reinforce this radical practice, use this lesson to teach children how to use a Bible concordance. A concordance is essentially an extensive index of the Bible, listing all the verses where each particular word appears. (Since different translations use different words, you must be sure to use a concordance that is made for the particular translation you are using.) Assign groups of children different words from the phrase 'eats with tax collectors and sinners'. Show them how to read the concordance references, including the book abbreviations. Remind them that they just need to look at the Gospel references. Ask each group to share how many stories they found where Jesus eats with tax collectors and sinners. Are there more in one Gospel than another? Are there more comments about this practice than actual stories of him doing it?

Watching them grow

Because the Bible often describes the inclusiveness or radicalness of Jesus as a man who eats with tax collectors and sinners, older teenagers are ready to learn more specifically what that characterization would have meant for the first hearers/readers of the Gospels.

- What does it mean that Jesus associates with those whom the world calls unclean, bad and immoral?
- Who would be 'tax collectors' in our world?
- Do we as Christians seek out these people to offer grace and love, or do we try to disassociate ourselves from them, just as Jesus' first followers did?

60 Jesus' entry to Jerusalem (Palm Sunday) (Matthew 21.1–11; Mark 11.1–10; Luke 19.28–40; John 12.12–19)

Palm Sunday marks the start of Holy Week as Jesus comes to the capital to face his impending fate. In some Gospels this is the first time in his ministry that Jesus even enters Jerusalem.

Planting the seed

Palm Sunday provides the perfect day of celebration to start conversations with children at home about Holy Week and these final days of Jesus' life. No matter how much you will participate as a family in community worship opportunities through Holy Week, you can still mark each day at home as a family. Choose a time each day that you will sit together as a family to read that day's story – Palm Sunday, Maundy Thursday, Good Friday, Easter Sunday. In talking about Palm Sunday you can talk with children about Jesus as the King of the Jews. He was a very different kind of king than people had expected, but you can still hear in the story the praise and elation that comes from the crowd and potentially from the stones as the people celebrate the coming of the Messiah to the city of David.

Feeding the soil

Similarly, Palm Sunday also provides an educational setting for guiding children through all the stories of Holy Week. In the congregation I served, we had a beautiful series of murals that ran the entire hallway of our education wing, retelling the stories from Palm Sunday through Easter. On Palm Sunday it was traditional to take each age group past all of the paintings, talking together with them about Jesus' last days. Even without a mural, you can create several stations representing the days of Holy Week and guide children through, using different sensory experiences to help them remember the day and the story. These kinds of activities are very helpful both for children who will not return to church for worship during Holy Week and for children who will.

Watching them grow

One of the starkest contrasts of Holy Week is between the crowds who sang and praised Jesus, welcoming him to Jerusalem on Sunday, and the crowd who called for his death on Friday. As students grow in their faith they can be introduced to some of the more complicated elements of this story, including the ways popular opinion swayed so dramatically during that week.

- Do we see ourselves in this crowd on Sunday?
- What about the crowd on Friday?
- Who was it who betrayed Jesus?
- Who was responsible for his death?

61 Jesus cleanses the Temple (Matthew 21.12–17; Mark 11.15–19; Luke 19.45–48; John 2.12–25)

In three of the Gospels, Jesus' triumphal entry into Jerusalem is followed by an assault on the Temple, where he casts out the money changers and the merchants selling animals for sacrifice, quoting Jeremiah 7.11: 'It is written, "My house shall be called a house of prayer"; but you are making it a den of robbers.'

Planting the seed

We paint a picture for our children of Jesus as pastoral and gracious, and these are accurate and good images to teach them. But children should also be taught that Jesus was a bit of a troublemaker. He upset a lot of powerful people through both his words and actions – especially when, as recorded in some versions of this story, he talked about tearing down the Temple and then rebuilding it. When children ask me why people wanted to kill Jesus, I often talk about his willingness to love all people and his courage to stand up to those who preached and practised hate. But we should not forget that he also challenged authority and had some harsh words to say to some of the religious leaders of his time. This is a vivid example of that kind of radical behaviour, which eventually led to his arrest.

Feeding the soil

We focus on the turning of the tables in this story and the clash of coins spilling all over the Temple floor, but just as vivid is the image of the sellers with their sacrificial animals being herded out of the Temple by an angry Jesus. Help students better understand what all the sellers were doing in the Temple in the first place. This was not just the market moved inside the doors of the Temple but rather an array of sacrificial animals for sale to pilgrims who had arrived in Jerusalem for the Passover feast. Read together the Old Testament instructions for the Passover sacrifice in Deuteronomy 16.1–8 and remind children of the sacrifice the Israelites made as they prepared to flee Egypt, marking their homes to keep them safe from the final plague.

Watching them grow

- Why does Jesus seem to act so out of character here?
- Is it actually out of character for him or do we just not read – or teach children – the more edgy stories of Jesus' ministry?
- What is the point of this outburst?
- Is he saying that these operations would be OK if they were located outside the Temple – just not inside its walls?
- What does this mean about how we handle money in the Church?
- Are there aspects of the world that we should 'keep out' of the Church?

62 The Last Supper (Maundy Thursday) (Matthew 26.17–30; Mark 14.12–30; Luke 22.7–23)

After a three-day break we meet up with Jesus and his disciples again in the Upper Room, where they are gathered to share in the

Passover meal and where Jesus 'institutes' the sacrament of Holy Communion.

Planting the seed

There are two aspects to Communion that we should teach children. First there is the *re-enacting* of this special moment that Jesus has with his disciples. This remembrance can be heavy and sad, when we remember what will happen later that evening. Each time we celebrate Communion we retell this story. But we should also teach children that Communion is a *rehearsal* for the meal that we will all share together with God and Jesus in the kingdom to come. In this way it is a meal of joy and celebration, not just a sad memorial.

Feeding the soil

When we think of the Last Supper it often conjures visions of Jesus washing the feet of his disciples. In fact this act of love and service only occurs in the Gospel of John (13.1–20). If you think they are willing, ask children to wash one another's feet. In some Christian traditions, men and women are divided for this kind of ritual. This may make children more comfortable as well. If this is too embarrassing or intimate for them, ask two adults to demonstrate the act for them. Having children turn down the activity because it is too intimate can actually be a great place to start a conversation about the humility Jesus was enacting by doing such a menial and intimate task for the disciples. Share with them that this would have been the job of a lowly servant in that culture.

Watching them grow

Included in this story as well is the interchange between Jesus and Judas. Older teenagers are ready to talk more about Judas and his decision to betray Jesus to the Sanhedrin. Jesus knows that Judas will betray him.

- Why doesn't he stop him?
- How do we understand Judas as a character in these stories?
- Was he destined to betray Jesus?
- Does he in some way represent the evil in each of us or the evil in the world?

63 Passion/crucifixion (Good Friday) (Matthew 26.36—27.61; Mark 14.32—15.47; Luke 22.39—23.56; John 18.1—19.42)

Jesus is arrested as he prays with his disciples in the garden. He is tried before the religious and political authorities and sentenced to death. Each Gospel tells it a little differently, and you will want to read each in preparation for talking together with children about Jesus' death.

Planting the seed

I admit that this might be the most difficult day/series of events to walk through with our children, and depending on what kind of Good Friday service your community offers, the age of a child should be taken into consideration when deciding whether or not to participate. By 8 or 9 years old, children should be able to sit with you through a service and understand the significance of Good Friday.

It is OK to tell children that these are sad stories that we don't like. The first time my own son sat with me on Good Friday, as the worship leaders did a dramatic reading of the Passion according to the Gospel of John he kept asking me, 'Who are these people yelling to crucify him? Why do they want him to die?' All I could come up with was that people make bad choices, they often don't understand what is happening around them, and that they didn't understand what they were doing.

Feeding the soil

I am not a fan at all of gratuitous re-enactments of the crucifixion of Jesus. The stories themselves are scary and painful enough without using overly dramatic ways to make them 'come alive' for children or young people. When we work with the same children over and over again in a congregational setting, we come to know them well enough to have a sense of what they can handle and how they will 'take on' such a difficult part of the Bible and our Christian tradition. Certainly I would not advocate whitewashing or sanitizing the story, but the atonement is no more real or effective the more graphically we choose to describe it.

Watching them grow

When they are older, you may want to help teenagers move beyond the too easily employed sentiment of 'Jesus dying for our sins'.

- Why did Jesus have to die?
- Did God abandon his son?
- Does God demand sacrifice?
- How are historical – and not so historical – anti-Semitic movements connected to Jesus' death?
- How do we describe those responsible for Jesus' death in accurate ways?

We can even get into the wide variety of metaphors that might describe the act of atonement, whether it be payment of a debt, the lamb led to the slaughter, Jesus taking our punishment for our sins or even Jesus taking on the sin of the world so that we would not suffer.

64 Resurrection (Easter) (Matthew 28; Mark 16; Luke 24.1–12; John 20.1–29)

Again, each Gospel brings a different flavour to these events, and taken together they give us a larger picture of how the earliest Christians understood the rising of Jesus from the tomb and appearing to the disciples.

Planting the seed

In my experience, conversations with children about the resurrection are some of the most neglected. Just like Christmas, Easter is wrapped up in a variety of cultural and materialistic traditions – at least in my US context. Gifts and candy/sweets from the Easter bunny can reach epic proportions; new clothes and shiny shoes can shift our focus away from the shocking significance of the Easter story.

The Gospel of Luke gives us one of the most beautiful post-resurrection stories, the Walk to Emmaus (24.13–35). As a way to make the idea of resurrection new for children, read together this story about the two travellers who are in despair over the death of Jesus. The two do a great job of summarizing their hopes for Jesus, their disappointment in his death, and then the anxiety they all felt in not understanding the resurrection. Jesus comes to them himself without their realizing it, and he comforts them in their grief and gives them hope for the future.

Feeding the soil

Because the four Gospels provide similar but unique versions of the resurrection story, looking at them together can be a great exercise for children in thinking more about the four being their own unique and fully contained versions of Jesus' life. Break the class into four groups, assigning each the specific chapter from one Gospel that tells the story of the resurrection. Give each group a large piece of paper and ask them to create an outline of the events as they happened, giving important details like where they occurred and which characters were involved. When they are done, hang all four outlines on the wall next to each other and use coloured masking tape or yarn to connect the similar elements of each story, creating a web across the Gospels. Highlight the items that are unique to each Gospel so that those details stand out among the similarities.

Watching them grow

When students are older we can start to talk together about the two kinds of resurrection the Bible teaches – not just Jesus' but the believer's as well (1 Cor. 15.12–34). How is Jesus' death made even more significant in his resurrection? For centuries before and after the death of Jesus, faithful Jewish and Christian martyrs have died for their beliefs. What happened with Jesus was different. The resurrection provides the theological belief that God's love for us is stronger even than death – that the destructive and evil forces we see witnessed on Good Friday are turned on their heads on Easter morning.

65 Ascension (Mark 16.19–20; Luke 24.50–53; Acts 1.6–11)

We have few details when it comes to what happens after Jesus' various post-resurrection appearances, except for two similar descriptions of him gathered with his disciples, raising his arms in blessing and then ascending into heaven.

Planting the seed

Who is Jesus for us today? As Christians we believe that Jesus returned to God after his resurrection. We talk to children about Jesus being in heaven, and often describe loved ones who have died as being 'in heaven' with Jesus as well. The ascension actually provides a background for a conversation on the incarnation – the idea that God became flesh in Jesus of Nazareth and lived here with human beings on earth at a specific moment in time. This coming was only temporary, and the ascension punctuates the gravity of God's love.

Feeding the soil

The story of the ascension of Jesus is so brief that it might help older children to read more about an early Christian understanding of it through the writings of Paul in the letter to the Ephesians. Supplement a conversation on the ascension with a reading from Ephesians 4.1–16. Talk through the beginning (the incarnation) and the end (the ascension) of Jesus' life and consider together how those two acts themselves show us God's love and Jesus' call on our lives as his disciples – as Paul begs us to lead a life worthy of the calling to which we have been called.

Watching them grow

- Who is Jesus supposed to be for us today?
- How are we connected to the historical figure who lived and died on this earth?
- How are we connected to a Jesus who after having risen from the dead now lives eternally with God in heaven?
- How do we experience the heavenly Jesus?
- What do modern people mean when they say they have a personal relationship with Jesus?
- How does one foster that kind of relationship?

11

The sayings and parables of Jesus

There are two aspects to teaching children about Jesus. One is teaching them what he did, which I have covered in the previous two chapters; the other is teaching them what he said. Sometimes the two are closely related, and when we seek to understand what Jesus said, we should always take into account what he was 'doing' when he said it. But there are certain key teachings that stand firmly on their own as foundational to the message of Jesus as presented by the four Gospels. Often Jesus used parables – fictional stories – to make a theological/ethical point. In other instances, through preaching, he made significant statements about who God is, who he himself is and who God's people are supposed to be.

An understanding of Jesus Christ as a teacher and an understanding of his *basic* teachings will help students as they get older to be ready to wrestle with the more *radical* teachings of Jesus, as they challenge our understanding of 'Christian' living today.

Below are five essential parables of Jesus and five of his essential teachings. These broadly represent not just who Jesus was but what he stood for.

66 The Beatitudes (Matthew 5.3–11)

Blessed are the poor in spirit, for theirs is the kingdom of heaven.
Blessed are those who mourn, for they will be comforted.

In the Beatitudes we have a summary of the upside-down-ness of the kingdom of God – that those the world calls blessed or fortunate are different from those God blesses and gives preference to. This collection of blessings comes at the very beginning of the Sermon on the Mount – the longest group of sayings and teachings found in the Gospels (see item 57).

Planting the seed

The beauty of the Beatitudes is in their poetry and repetitive liturgical style. They can be easily included in a family's mealtime or bedtime prayer routine. Their rhythm and simplicity make them ideal to recite with children. Take the next step and talk to children about each of these blessings:

- What does it mean to be 'poor in spirit'?
  - To be hungry?
  - To be persecuted?
  - To be a peacemaker?
  - To mourn?
- Are these normally things we experience as blessings?
- What does it mean to be blessed by God?

Feeding the soil

While you should be sure to teach the Beatitudes in their entirety for students, focusing on what it means for Christians to be peacemakers – 'Blessed are the peacemakers, for they will be called children of God' – might provide for the most fruitful conversation in the classroom.

We tell students all the time that they are beloved children of God. If we read this verse backwards, then, what obligation do we have as children of God to be peacemakers in our world? Ask children to talk about what it means to be a peacemaker in their families.

- What does it mean to be a peacemaker at school?
- What does it mean to be a peacemaker in their local community or global community?

Use this moment to introduce them to peacemakers from history or current events.

Watching them grow

Beyond the poetry and the rhythm of these verses there is a radicalness to Jesus' teachings.

- What would the world look like if we also blessed and honoured these types of people?
- What does it mean that the world's preferences and God's preferences are different?
- Why would God want us to be persecuted?
- Do you think you would ever be persecuted for your faith?
- Do you see yourself in this list?
- Who are some of the people, in our modern world, that this list includes?

67 'Love your enemies and pray for those who persecute you' (Matthew 5.43–44)

The next four teachings in this list deal with love and the way Jesus described our call to love others. This first one might be the trickiest and the most difficult: the call to love our enemies. As we teach children about the life of Jesus and the message of the Gospel we should emphasize his love not just for the unfortunate and the outcast but also for his enemies. Even unto death Jesus is portrayed in the Gospels as having no animosity for those who would kill him. In a world where so many people are defined by who they call enemy, this is an essential tenet of the teachings of Christ.

Planting the seed

I had a friend at church growing up who was never allowed to say that she hated someone. Her parents taught her to say that she didn't like a person but she was never to use the word 'hate'. 'Hate' and 'enemy' are strong words, and as much as we might try to keep them out of our children's vocabulary they will inevitably experience these kinds of feelings and difficult relationships. What is interesting to me is that Jesus never says that we shouldn't have enemies or that if we live by the law we will not have difficult relationships. For him they are inevitable. It is how we respond to the hate that shapes who we are as Christians.

We teach this lesson to our children when they come home complaining of bullies or just plain difficult children in their lives. We tell them to forgive people who hurt them, to avoid people they don't like and to look for silver linings in bad situations. That is the easy part. More difficult is how we model this 'rule' for them in our own lives.

- Do they overhear us talking about others in hateful or less than charitable ways?
- Do we inadvertently teach them that those who disagree with us are not to be respected?

Feeding the soil

We reinforce this teaching with children in our communities each time the call to pray for our enemies and those who persecute us is actually put into practice. When children hear us pray in worship or in class, do they hear us ask God to consider our enemies, those whom it is difficult to love? Simply making a practice of teaching children to pray for their enemies is the most practical way to make this essential teaching a part of their identity as Christians.

Watching them grow

Older students will be able to talk more deeply about the events of Holy Week and why it seems like Jesus is unwilling to fight back or become embittered by his circumstances

- Who are our personal enemies?
- Why do we identify them that way?
- How can we love those who intentionally hurt us?
- What if the world operated in this way?
- What would be missing in the world – war, political divisions, brokenness in families?

68 'Do to others as you would have them do to you' (Matthew 7.12)

I believe that most parents, even outside of a Christian context, teach their children the Golden Rule. It is just basic human decency. Don't do something to someone else that you wouldn't want to have done to you.

Planting the seed

While the Golden Rule may be essential to the development of 'natural' laws, our children are not born to follow it naturally. In

many ways children, by their nature, are self-centred and nar-
cissistic. This doesn't reflect poorly on them as human beings, it is
just part of their natural development of self. But as parents we
are called to help them move through this developmental stage
by giving them a paradigm for their lives. Children can understand
the Golden Rule long before they are able to follow it. While many
children can exhibit selfless acts of generosity, they can also be short-
sighted and focus on self-preservation more often than we care to
admit.

Teaching them this 'rule' must inevitably address the reality that
showing kindness and compassion, that sharing and giving, that
forgiving and forgetting all come with a measure of sacrifice on
our own part. We teach our children not just to treat others the way
we would want to be treated but to be willing to sacrifice for others
as we hope others will sacrifice for us.

Feeding the soil

As I mentioned back in Chapter 5, I encourage leaders and children
to create community 'rules' for their class or fellowship groups, but
when children are younger they need to be provided with the language
we use as Christians when we talk about how we treat other people.
In conversations with children about their behaviour specifically in
the class, the Golden Rule provides the framework for explaining why
we listen when others are talking, why we take turns, why we share
supplies and toys, why we go out of our way to include everyone
in our activities and why we practise hospitality to guests and new
students.

Watching them grow

Older students are just getting to the point of being self-aware and
able to step seriously outside of their own behaviour and talk about
why they do the things they do.

- Why do we treat others badly, whether through gossip or lying,
  exclusion or even mean-spiritedness, when we would never want
  to be treated that way?
- Could you go a whole day only treating others as you would want
  to be treated?
- When is this easy and when is this harder?

69 'Love the Lord your God . . . love your neighbour as yourself' (Matthew 22.37–40)

This law of love that Jesus quotes immediately before telling the Parable of the Good Samaritan is a reference to the Old Testament passage often called the *Shema*, found in the book of Deuteronomy (see Chapter 5). Jesus adds to this a summary of the rest of the law: that we are called to love our neighbours as we love ourselves. In putting these two Commandments of love together, Jesus connects our desire to love God with our willingness to follow God's law – that by following the law and loving our neighbours we are also showing our love for God. They cannot be separated.

Planting the seed

We use the word 'love' very casually these days, and so when we talk with children about what it means to love God and to remember that God loves us, it is helpful to define what that kind of love is all about. In this summary of law and love, Jesus actually calls us to three expressions of love – love for God, love for ourselves, love for our neighbour. When we talk with our children about how much God loves them, we should remind them that God's gift of love compels a loving response. We show our love for God when we treat ourselves with love and when we show love to those around us. Each time we love our neighbour, God receives that as our love for him as well.

Feeding the soil

Since this verse from Matthew is a 'summary' of the law, it is most effectively introduced in the classroom as such, which is why it works well to teach it in tandem with the Ten Commandments. We teach the laws of Moses as individual descriptions of behaviour and faith expression but we should also help children understand the pattern they follow.

It can be as simple as providing students with each of the Ten Commandments written on their own index card, and asking them to sort them between an expression of loving God and loving our neighbour. As they assign each one, ask them to explain how that particular command is an expression of love.

Watching them grow

- How does our identity as Christians have an impact on the way we live in our communities?
- How do you treat your actual neighbours in your neighbourhood?
- What does it mean to be a good neighbour?
- Can someone be a neighbour across geographic boundaries?
- How does loving other people around us show our love for God?
- What do you think God expects from us in how we treat other people, especially people who are not like us?

70 'For God so loved the world that he gave his only Son, so that everyone who believes in him may not perish but may have eternal life' (John 3.16)

I actually went around and around before I included this verse in my list. There are so many other expressions in the Gospel of John of Jesus' work on earth and our relationship to him as our saviour – I am the vine you are the branches; I am the way the truth and the life; I am the good shepherd who lays down his life for his sheep. Keep in mind that this list in this book of 100 essentials is not meant to set the limit on what we teach our children but rather the very minimum to which they should be exposed.

This particular – and often quoted – verse is taken from the story of Jesus meeting at night with the Jewish leader Nicodemus. There is no reason to teach this verse to children outside of the context from which it comes. Nicodemus has real questions about who Jesus is and what he is calling his followers to do and believe. He and Jesus have a fascinating conversation about being born again, and ironically, though John 3.16 is used as a definitive description of the atoning work of Christ, eight verses before it Jesus describes the spirit of God as working in ways that the human mind and heart cannot fully comprehend.

Planting the seed

Children are very good at parroting back the sentiment that Jesus died to save them from their sins, but can hardly articulate what that actually means, let alone what sins they could possibly have committed to warrant such a dramatic punishment. Yes, it is important to teach children about Christ's sacrifice and the ways that affirming faith in Jesus Christ as our saviour is a part of being a Christian. But it is also important to be willing to share with our children that the ways that God works are often beyond our understanding. Just as Nicodemus struggled to understand, so do we all at some point struggle to comprehend fully the work done on our behalf through Christ. This verse is most helpful when it is taught as an exploration of faith rather than a litmus test of salvation.

Feeding the soil

The story of Nicodemus is often neglected in a regular rotation of children's Bible stories. His narrative 'mirror' in the Gospel of John – the Samaritan woman at the well – is also much neglected in the classroom (she makes this list at item 58). In the spirit of teaching children to look for connections and patterns in the biblical text, these are two stories that can, when taught together, encourage children to examine more subtle details in them.

Children can identify both the similarities and differences in these conversations. For example, both involve just Jesus and one other person – but one happens in private and the other in public.

- How do we understand the meaning of John 3.16 when we read it in light of Jesus' revelation to the Samaritan woman that those who drink the water that he offers will never be thirsty?
- What does it mean that we will never die?
- What does it mean that we will never be thirsty?

Watching them grow

Older students should bring to conversations about the atoning work of God through Jesus Christ not just the stories of Jesus but the larger story of Scripture and salvation from the Old to New Testaments. Then they can struggle with these questions:

- Is there something in your life you would die for?
- Is there someone in your life you would die for?
- How can we honour the death of Jesus without glorifying his suffering and the violence of Good Friday?
- If Jesus died to give us eternal life, what does that mean for us today – do those who die in the faith immediately go to heaven?
- How does what Jesus taught during his life relate to the meaning of his death?

- What if my faith waivers?
- What if I sometimes struggle to believe?
- Does that mean that I am not saved?
- What does it mean that God loves the world – not just particular people?

71 The Good Samaritan (Luke 10.25–37)

The law of loving one's neighbour is found in the book of Leviticus and thus at the foundation of the moral and ritual laws of the Jewish people. In the parable of the Good Samaritan a man is attacked as he travels, and while he lies hurt on the side of the road not one but two men pass him by without stopping to help: first a priest; then a Levite. It is only when a Samaritan comes across the injured man that he is helped. The moral of the story is that it was the Samaritan – someone viewed as outside the Jewish community – who acted as the true neighbour.

Planting the seed

Because most of these parables can be found in a children's picture Bible, you can start teaching them from a very early age. When reading any of them with children, make sure to explain that these were stories Jesus told, not stories of things that actually happened. It is a simple distinction to make, even though most children's Bibles don't take the time.

As you reflect on this parable with your children, ask them to tell you:

- Why do they think the first two men wouldn't stop to help?
- Why did the last man stop?
- Who do they think Jesus wants us to be like?
- When have they helped someone who was hurt?
- When did they not help someone in need?

Share your own experiences of acting like a neighbour to someone in need or a time when you were helped yourself.

Feeding the soil

Beyond teaching this parable to children in class, congregations and communities should also teach by example by helping those in need and reaching out to the neighbour in our midst. In the very way we welcome people into our sanctuaries and church buildings we are teaching our children what it means to love one's neighbour.

In my congregation we experienced at the same time both a dramatic increase in the use of our modest food bank and the completion of a multi-million-dollar building renovation that included a newly created fellowship/reception area. For months after the renovation was complete, guests to the food bank were ushered past it and asked to sit in folding chairs in the hallway to reduce wear and tear on this newly created space. Eventually, through the wisdom of one of our deacons, the church realized that keeping this space closed and clean was not as important as providing comfort and hospitality to those in need.

Children frequently volunteer with their parents in distributing food to guests, and each time a child invites someone in need to sit in the same space that they use for community fellowship each Sunday it teaches them that caring for their neighbour is the highest value in their church.

Watching them grow

Many of Jesus' teachings relate directly to his interpretation of the laws of the Old Testament.

- How do we as Christians still follow some of the laws in the book of Leviticus today?

We can talk about what it meant for the hero of the story to be a Samaritan.

- Who were the Samaritans in the ancient world, and why were they outsiders?
- Who are the 'Samaritans' in our world today?

We can also talk more about a theological understanding of the word 'neighbour'.

- Is a neighbour just someone who lives near me, or anyone who might be in need?
- How do we as modern Christians love our neighbours?

72 The Lost Sheep and Coin (Luke 15.1–10)

The two stories are very similar: one of a shepherd who leaves behind his flock of 99 sheep to find the one that is lost; the other of a woman who, having nine coins, searches her house relentlessly to find the lost tenth coin. Jesus is making the point that his work – and God's work – is not just concerned with the found but intentionally focuses on the lost.

Planting the seed

Both of these parables are very simple and easy for children to understand. However, living in a disposable culture, it might be difficult for them to appreciate the determination the shepherd and the woman demonstrate. If my son only lost 1 per cent of his coloured pencils at school he would be pretty satisfied with his retention rate. Stress that God – the shepherd and the woman – is not satisfied with 99 per cent, but is willing to take the extra effort to make sure that everyone is found. What is something in their life that they would only be satisfied if they kept 100 per cent of? Family? Friends? This is the same way God feels about us.

Feeding the soil

These two parables lend themselves incredibly well to dramatic play. The simplicity of the storyline and the lack of 'dialogue' means that after reading through the story, even young children should be able to take on the part of the shepherd or the woman and act out the tasks of seeking, finding and celebrating.

The next parable in our list – and in the Gospel of Luke – is that of the Prodigal Son. These three parables fit together as a continuous illustration of God's willingness to welcome home and even to seek out those who have become lost and separated from him. Use these two shorter parables in the classroom to help children review the much longer one of the Prodigal Son. Once they know that parable it should be easy for them to identify the same priority for grace and forgiveness in these two shorter parables.

Watching them grow

Young people should be assured of God's relentless pursuit of us even when we have gone astray. God is not locked inside the church waiting for us to find him there. Rather God actively looks for us, and for all sinners, when we are lost. Parables can paint vivid pictures of who God is. Our language for God is limited to our human understanding. Parables like these can give us more varied images of God to help us better understand the nature of God.

- What are the qualities of a shepherd that make him like God?
- What does it mean to imagine God as a woman cleaning her home?

73 The Prodigal Son (Luke 15.11–32)

A man has two sons: one asks for his share of his inheritance early from his father and goes off and spends it frivolously; the other remains at home, faithful to his father's household. The wayward son, upon returning home, is welcomed back with open arms and a celebration far beyond what he deserves. The faithful son becomes bitter and struggles to understand why his wayward brother has been rewarded despite such bad behaviour, when he himself is the one who deserves a celebration.

Planting the seed

From the start, point out how unusual it would have been for this younger son to take his inheritance and leave home at a young age, before his father had died. Because we don't live in the same cultural context, give children examples from their lives about things they might do to turn their back on their family.

You can ask them if they have ever done something so bad they wondered if their parents would forgive them. How did it feel when they were forgiven? How have they felt when their brother or sister did something wrong and then was forgiven? It has become common to refer to this parable not as the parable of the Prodigal Son but as the parable of the Two Brothers. In this story both brothers react to the father's act of grace and forgiveness, and very often we are in the position of the older brother who is indignant at his father's willingness to forgive.

Feeding the soil

Even at an early age children can be taught to read the Bible with a narrative sensibility. Much of Scripture can be understood and interpreted from the perspective of how the story has been told, how characters are described and how dialogue is shaped. Start out with these kinds of simple stories and ask children intentional questions about why Jesus would have told the story the way he did. Which character do they most relate to? The father? The younger son? The older son?

Because this parable is mostly about the relationships between the three primary characters, you can use artistic interpretations of these relationships to help children understand the way the characters interact. Rembrandt's interpretation of the parable, his painting *The Return of the Prodigal Son*, is one of the most ubiquitous images of the story (and very easily found online). But even a 'bad' illustration of the parable can give the children the freedom to disagree with an artist's interpretation. Children can then be asked to create their own artistic version of the story, paying particular attention to how these three family members relate to each other.

Watching them grow

How do we understand the grace of God? God's love seems foolish as God continues to welcome home and embrace even those who have turned their backs on him. How does it feel to be that older brother who always does everything right and never feels appreciated? Even 2,000 years ago people understood sibling rivalry and the complicated nature of human relationships. The father was always there waiting with arms open for the son to return, and we can connect this story to the lost sheep and the lost coin – God will go to great lengths to make sure we come home safe.

74 The Sower (Matthew 13.1–9)

Jesus explains why he teaches in parables by telling *yet another parable* – that of a farmer who sows his fields in a somewhat haphazard way. In the process, seeds land in a variety of places, not all of them promising: on the edge of the field; on rocky ground; in the thorns; and then on good soil – the only place it can take root, grow and flourish. Interestingly, this is one of the few parables for which the Gospels provide a detailed explanation of its meaning. The seed represents the Word; the different kinds of ground represent people's varying levels of willingness or ability to receive/hear the Word.

Planting the seed

One of the earliest lessons children learn in school is what it takes for a seed to grow – light, air, water and soil. Take away any one of these and your bean sprout is leggy, limp or even non-existent. Remind them of this basic lesson of botany and see if they can make the connection to the different types of soil Jesus describes in the parable.

Talk to children about when in the course of a day or a week they themselves are most receptive to learning. What do they do to be ready for school and to make sure they are good soil to learn from their teachers? Get a good night's rest? Have a healthy breakfast? Make sure they have the things they need for school in their pencil cases and school bags? In a way this is what Jesus is talking about as well. How can we prepare ourselves to be ready to learn from him and to help our faith grow?

Feeding the soil

This parable lends itself very well to reproducing the same science experiment of growing a seed at church that the children may have done in school already. Ask them to use the lessons they have learned from science to help explain why different types of soil might be more or less receptive to growth.

Take children outside the church building to look around and see different types of soil and ground around the church. Certainly even within a few blocks they should be able to identify some of the same 'types' of soil that Jesus describes.

- What do they see growing in these places?
- Where are the places where nothing is able to take root?

Watching them grow

- How do we as Christians prepare ourselves to be that good ground?
- Does that include studying Scripture faithfully, praying regularly, attending worship?
- What are some of the things that we do in our lives that keep us from having ears that can hear the word of God?
- Why does Jesus speak in parables so often?
- Why is it that sometimes the meaning of Scripture seems to elude us?
- Why in the rest of this passage does Jesus so clearly state that there are some people who just will not and cannot understand what it is he is trying to teach them?
- Shouldn't there be some way that he is able to break through and connect with all people?

75 The Mustard Seed (Matthew 13.31–32)

The kingdom of heaven is like a mustard seed that someone took and sowed in his field; it is the smallest of all the seeds, but when it has grown it is the greatest of shrubs and becomes a tree, so that the birds of the air come and make nests in its branches.

This particular parable is one of several labelled the 'kingdom parables', in which Jesus uses object lessons to describe the nature of the kingdom of God.

Planting the seed

It is possible that children will never see a mustard seed in their life, unless you intentionally show them one. It is even more unlikely they will ever see a mustard tree or bush. It has become common to translate this parable into that of the acorn and the oak tree. Showing children the small acorn next to the mighty oak tree illustrates the same point – that though the work of God seems small at the start, it has the capability of becoming exponentially large. Imagine what the kingdom of God might be like. Brainstorm together what the world would be like if God made all of the rules.

- How would people behave?
- How would resources be shared?
- How would people take care of each other?

Feeding the soil

Have children make a list together of the small things that any of us can do to help make a big change in the world.

- What simple acts of kindness can grow into new ways of being community together?
- What simple acts of conservation can help to protect the earth?
- What simple acts of responsibility can help their family be more productive?

Jesus talks about the small glimpses of the kingdom of God helping that kingdom grow into a large movement. Help children connect their behaviour to acts of kingdom building. This would be a great moment to introduce to them the prayer of Teresa of Ávila – 'Christ has no body now, but yours . . . Yours are the hands with which Christ blesses the world.' Have them trace around their small hands and ask them to imagine what great things Christ can do through such small hands.

Watching them grow

- Is the kingdom of God anything like an earthly kingdom?
- What does it mean that it can start with the smallest seed?
- What might Jesus have meant the seed to represent?
  - Him?
  - Us?
  - Scripture?
  - Faith?
- When we pray, 'Thy kingdom come, thy will be done', what are we asking God to do through us?

12

The Early Church

———•◦•———

The Christian experience is rooted in community from its very start. To be a Christian outside of community means losing an essential part of how the Bible models faith expression and the practices of faith.

Unfortunately Confirmation Sunday sometimes takes on an air of graduation instead of commencement as students – and parents – treat it as a day of liberation from the burdens of Sunday school. Confirmation really should be considered a day of binding – binding one's heart and mind to Jesus Christ and binding one's expression and experience of faith to the community.

When I start the confirmation process with students we always read from Paul's first letter to the Corinthians, chapter 12, as he describes our connectedness as individual members in the singular body of Christ:

> Indeed, the body does not consist of one member but of many . . .
> And if the ear were to say, 'Because I am not an eye, I do not belong to the body', that would not make it any less a part of the body . . . But as it is, God arranged the members in the body, each one of them, as he chose. If all were a single member, where would the body be? As it is, there are many members, yet one body. (1 Cor. 12.14–20)

By starting in this way we are mindful of how each of these students will find their place, express their unique gifts and learn from those who are different, as members not just of one congregation but within the entire body of Christ.

As students continue to build on the foundations that have been laid, our conversations about the history of the Church, the way the Bible guides our relationships within the Church and the ways the Church engages with the world can be deeper and broader and have a more significant impact on students' ability and willingness to identify themselves as members of the body of Christ when they have already connected to these essential elements of our Christian life.

76 The gift of the Holy Spirit (Acts 2)

Jesus' disciples are gathered together in a home 50 days after Easter when the Holy Spirit comes upon them as a mighty wind and lights upon their heads like tongues of fire. They leave to go out into the city to preach. They find that even though the very cosmopolitan crowd speaks a variety of languages, they all seem to understand the disciples speaking in Aramaic. The Bible says that 3,000 people were baptized that day, which is why we call Pentecost the 'birthday' of the Church. (See also item 84, where I talk about how we celebrate the season of Pentecost as a worshipping community.)

Planting the seed

The story of Pentecost can teach children the ways Christian faith has spread around the world. If you have a world map or a globe at home, help them find Israel on it. They will probably not be able to find the other ancient cities mentioned in the passage, but you can explain that these people represented Jews from a larger geographic area surrounding Jerusalem, North Africa and Asia Minor. Then ask them to find their own home on the map or globe. Imagine together how the message the disciples preached that day made it all the way to where you are living today. Who carried this good news? Explain how generation after generation of Christians have repeated this same message in different languages all over the world. Pentecost may be the birthday of the Church and Jerusalem its birthplace, but the Church lives and grows all over the world today.

Feeding the soil

Language and the Bible has a fascinating history. From Hebrew to Greek to Latin, the language of faith is always shifting and growing as the Church grows around the world. When you study this story of Pentecost with children, share with them Bibles in different modern languages. If you are not able to find multiple Bibles it is easy to pick a particular passage in German, French, Spanish and so on, find it online and print it off. In many churches in the USA we have the story of Pentecost read in different languages in worship on that day, but doing this activity in class can allow children to reflect on the true miracle of Pentecost – not that the disciples were able to speak in so many different languages but that the people were all able to *hear* in their own language.

Help children think about what it would be like to be in a church community where most people spoke languages different from yours. Help them also consider how the Holy Spirit helps us listen to each other – about our feelings, our faith, our hopes and our fears – even if we are all speaking the same language. That ability or willingness to listen to one another is one of the things that makes the Church so strong.

Watching them grow

Though Jesus and his disciples were Jewish there was a point at which the followers of Jesus began to structure their lives and their community in a different way from that heritage. We talk with older students both about the way the Church developed from this point on and the ways that we still today rely on the work of the Holy Spirit to inspire our life together as Church through the reading of Scripture, worship, preaching and the sacraments.

77 The conversion (call) of Paul (Acts 9)

There are several aspects of Paul's story to which students should be introduced to provide a foundation for later exploration. The story of his 'conversion' – a conversion not 'from' Judaism but 'to' the messianic Jewish sect later called 'Christian' – gives a sense of his call to Christian ministry and the development of the Early Church. Paul – or rather Saul as he is known in Judea – is a Pharisee who is persecuting the first Christian converts. During a trip to Damascus he is struck by a blinding light and hears a voice that says, 'Saul, Saul, why do you persecute me?' The voice identifies himself as Jesus and instructs him to travel to Damascus. There he will find a man named Ananias who will care for him. Paul takes up preaching the good news of Jesus Christ, and his lifelong ministry of evangelism and church planting around the Mediterranean begins.

Planting the seed

The story of Paul's conversion can help us introduce to children the reality that some of the first Christians were persecuted for their faith. Since most of us live in places where either Christianity is the majority religion or where religious freedom is practised, it might be hard for them to consider that there was a time when Christians were arrested and even killed for expressing faith in Jesus Christ. Older children can have a conversation about the ways Christians have unfortunately also been the persecutors, either of one another or of those who practise non-Christian religions. (See Chapter 15 for more on how to have those conversations with children.)

Feeding the soil

Some stories from the Bible lend themselves to drama and theatre better than others. Help children who are kinesthetic learners – in that they learn best through movement – engage with this story by dividing the biblical text into narration and dialogue and asking children to take turns acting out the story. Encourage them to experiment with how Paul might have changed because of his conversion. Is his voice different? Does he walk differently? How does he find his way to Ananias? They can also experiment with what the voice of Jesus might sound like. By acting this story out they can experience the very physical way that Ananias restores Paul's sight. The story is short enough that they would be able to act it out several times. Use different modern translations of the story to see if it prompts different theatrical interpretations.

Watching them grow

So much of what we believe about Christian theology and the Christian life comes not from the Gospels but from the writings of Paul (see item 78). As students come to understand the teachings of Paul they should also have a sense of his life and ministry. When they come with this story of his conversion under their belt, students can be introduced to Paul's struggles as a Christian himself, his debates within the Christian community and why so much of the New Testament is dedicated to his writings. They can also learn how to read the stories of Paul found in Acts alongside the theology of Paul found in his letters.

78 The journeys and letters of Paul

There are 21 letters – or 'epistles' as we sometimes call them – in the New Testament. Scholars and church leaders have debated which ones were written by whom. The majority of them – no matter where you fall on the authorship issue – were written by the Apostle Paul. These letters give us significant insight into both the ecclesiological (church) and theological (beliefs) debates in the early Christian communities: the expectations that were put on Early Church leadership; how the laws of the Old Testament were either applied or abandoned; how the Early Church slowly developed unique worship traditions. Paul travelled along the Mediterranean as far as Rome, teaching people about Jesus. Part of that work meant also teaching them how to shape their life together and how to deal with conflict and disagreements within the community.

Planting the seed

I have a hard time finding ways to engage children in the theological writings of Paul. Many of the concepts are a little too abstract, and he is often struggling to resolve a theological 'problem' that children can't relate to just yet.

But there is one piece of Pauline theology that we actually expose children to when they attend weddings. 1 Corinthians 13 is a standard at many Christian weddings, even though the elevated description of love that Paul paints has nothing to do with romantic love or even love between spouses. The love he describes is the kind that should flourish within the Christian community. While you are looking for ways to occupy children in the midst of a wedding service, help them look up this love passage from Paul. Talk to them about the ways we love people we are not married to or who are not even in our family.

- Can we have this same kind of love for all people?
- Would the world be a different place if people tried to live up to this standard of love?

Feeding the soil

Help children wrap their heads around the ministry of Paul by allowing them to walk in his footsteps. Create an oversized map of the

Mediterranean world on the floor of a classroom with masking tape, which is easy to remove if not left in place too long. Using such a map of Paul's journeys you can help children travel from Jerusalem to Asia Minor, the Greek isles all the way to Rome. Most children's study Bibles will include a map of Paul's journeys that shows how he travelled from city to city. I tend to strive for a general sense of the geography and simplify the topographic details of the shorelines. Make sure to label the Mediterranean Sea as well as regions like Galatia, Macedonia, Judea and Greece. As children travel, have them read out loud small and iconic passages from the letter that he sent to the Christians in that place (for example, Rom. 8.28–30; 1 Cor. 12.4–11; Gal. 1.3–10; Eph. 6.1–4; Phil. 2.5–11; Col. 3.12–17; Thess. 5.12–22). This will give them a taste for his writing and theology as well as a greater understanding of how Christianity grew in the first century.

Watching them grow

What does it really means to be a part of a community? Sometimes that means arguments, conflicts, change and disagreements. Together in class we can look at the debates the first Christians had as they tried to figure out what it meant to share a common faith and even sometimes a common purse and life together. Confirmation is not about painting a rosy picture of the Church but about equipping young people to be engaged in the choices that really matter in the life of the community, to discern when conflicts and division are happening over non-essential elements of the Christian life and not to be discouraged when there is conflict in their church experience.

79 The differences between Jews and Gentiles

There is no other topic I introduce in confirmation class that causes more confusion and consternation for students than the explanation of the distinctions between Jews and Gentiles in the first generation of Christian converts. I know they usually come understanding what it means to be a Jew. What I think they get caught up on is the idea that there would have been an actual name for anyone who was not a Jew – or what we refer to as a Gentile (our word comes from the Latin translation of the Greek and Jewish words used in the Bible for non-Jews, which mean 'nations'). It may be because they them-selves *are* Gentiles and never knew it. I am not sure. It is certainly not a complex concept, and one that if introduced early and often should not be as traumatic as it winds up being.

Planting the seed

In Christ Jesus you are all children of God through faith. As many of you as were baptized into Christ have clothed yourselves with Christ. There is no longer Jew or Greek, there is no longer slave or free, there is no longer male and female; for all of you are one in Christ Jesus.

(Gal. 3.26–28)

These verses from Paul's letter to the Galatians provide a means to talk to children about how within the Church we celebrate our diversity, but also don't use differences to treat people differently or say that one or the other is more valuable in the Christian community. They will understand that there is a difference between men and women, and so you can explain to them that within the Church there were also people who were born Jews and people who were born outside of the Jewish community. Yet despite these differences they both called each other Christians.

Feeding the soil

The nativity stories also provide fodder for introducing the ways the Bible talks about those who were outside of the Jewish community. While in the Gospel of Luke the prophet Simeon sings of Jesus' role as the bringer of light to the Gentiles, it is the story in Matthew of the Wise Men's visit to the Holy Family that provides the best illustration for how the early Christians saw the potential for the gospel message to reach into the Gentile world.

Instead of focusing in on their identity as astrologers or magi, help children think of the Wise Men as Gentiles – people who would have been outside of the Jewish tradition. Even these people, who it seems would not have had reason to welcome the Messiah, come to worship him. Talk about how these nativity stories help us understand how the first Christians wanted to describe Jesus. Matthew's description of Jesus' birth introduces this idea that Jesus' message will reach further out into the world of the Gentiles.

Watching them grow

The Early Church wrestled with how to maintain a Jewish identity while also opening the community to Gentiles.

- What traditions were retained?
- What practices were set aside?
- What was lost and what was gained?
- What does the Bible tell us about what it means to practise our faith, to identify ourselves as disciples and to spread the good news outside of our community?

80 The book of Revelation

I am not sure that the book of Revelation really fits in this group of five, when we think of it in terms of how confirmation helps to shape students in their understanding of the Christian community both today and over the past 2,000 years. But it does relate to how we understand Christianity to be in relationship with the world around it. The Revelation to John is often described as 'apocalyptic literature', a type of writing in which otherworldly beings reveal secrets about the future and/or the cosmos to ordinary mortals. Revelation describes the vision of John on the island of Patmos and describes the coming of Jesus Christ again to the earth and all that goes into the final judgement of the world.

Planting the seed

We have a lot of names for Jesus – Messiah, Emmanuel, Good Shepherd, Prince of Peace, Lamb of God. One that we take from Revelation is Jesus as the Alpha and Omega. There are not many parts of Revelation I would snuggle up on the couch to read with a child, but Revelation 21.1–7 provides a beautiful description of the world to come and can introduce children to the language of Alpha and Omega, the first and last letters of the Greek alphabet. What would it mean if we called Jesus the A and the Z? Show them what the Alpha and Omega letters look like, and point out those symbols to them at church and other religious spaces.

Feeding the soil

Along the same lines as the conversations above, this idea of Jesus as the Alpha and Omega gives children a chance to explore and experiment with religious symbols they can find both in their own church and in religious art.

Take them on an exploration of your church and sanctuary looking for other symbolic representations of Jesus and images of faith. Might they find a Chi Rho (the first two Greek letters in the name 'Christ'), or maybe an artistic rendering of 'INRI' (a Latin acronym for 'Jesus of Nazareth, King of the Jews')? And how about 'IHS' (the first three Greek letters in the name 'Jesus')? Quite often children see these acronyms and symbols all around them, and no one takes the time to explain what they mean.

Watching them grow

We don't spend much time at all on Revelation in my confirmation class. But here is one of the reasons I think students should be aware of it and have a general understanding of what it is, even if they have never actually read it themselves. Confirmation has to be a place where students can bring their questions. Many of them have not had a safe place like this before where they can be pretty sure that they are going to get an honest answer. It is totally within the realm of possibility that in a group of students, one of them has been reading through Revelation and is either a little freaked out by it or maybe just intrigued. It would be very normal for them then to ask about it in class. Of all of the questions in this book that can be tackled in confirmation class, the most important ones are those that students bring with them to class heavy on their hearts.

13

Worship, sacraments and the life of the congregation

The worship life of a congregation is the place where so much of what we 'work on' when we prepare students to become adult members of the Christian community is actually 'worked out' in the life of the church: prayer, the Bible, sin and forgiveness, balance between lay and ordained leadership, mission and stewardship – just to name a few.

As much time as I might spend with a student of any age talking about what it means to be an active part of a worshipping community, they will actually learn more by watching and accompanying the other adults in their families. That is the premise of the last two items in this chapter, which I hope will give you ideas and encouragement to talk with your children about what it means *to you* to be a part of your church community.

81 Advent

Advent is a month-long season of holy waiting as we prepare to celebrate the birth of Jesus Christ at Christmas. Typically this season is marked with the colour blue or purple and is characterized most vividly for children by the weekly lighting of the four Advent candles.

Planting the seed

Advent provides myriad opportunities for talking with our children about the meaning of Christmas. Advent calendars and Advent devotionals help to mark each day of waiting, but no matter how we try to slow down long enough to teach children the true message of

Christmas, we can still be outmanoeuvred by the materialism of the modern Christmas season.

My husband frequently reminds me that during his childhood, though the family nativity set was always set up in early December, the baby Jesus was never added to the scene until Christmas Day. This is a very visible way for children to be reminded of the anticipation of the season, and is a great conversation starter. Talk with your children about the importance of waiting, reminding them that we are not just waiting for Christmas but for the coming of Jesus again to the earth.

Feeding the soil

Most congregations mark time in Advent by lighting a candle on the community Advent wreath each week in worship as a symbol of the coming of the light of the world among us during the darkness of these winter days.

Children love being included in this community tradition, and each year in my church we tried to include children and young people in different ways. Some years each week's candle would be lit by a family who had recently welcomed a child themselves. Some Advents, confirmation students and their mentors took turns lighting the candles. One year children lit the candles and read the liturgy with their adult prayer partners.

Helping to light the Advent candles can be the very first moment a child is invited to lead the community in worship and the first step on their journey to being personally invested in community worship traditions.

Watching them grow

We have been waiting, along with the rest of the Christian community, for 2,000 years for Christ to return.

- What will it be like when Jesus comes again?
- How will we know?
- Will it be like the book of Revelation?
- We have been waiting so long; will we ever give up waiting?

A great way to start these conversations is to look together with young people at the lectionary readings assigned for the first week of Advent each year, which focus not on the birth of the Christ child but on the vision for Christ come again to earth.

82 Lent

Lent is another season of preparation as Christians journey along with Jesus to Jerusalem, the cross, and the resurrection. Lent is marked by the colour purple – a reminder of the cloth that was draped on Jesus before his death. In previous generations this was also a time of preparation for the baptism of new converts. This season lasts 40 days, not counting Sundays. These 40 days are reminiscent of Jesus' 40 days tempted in the wilderness, the 40 days of the flood in Genesis or even the 40 years that the Israelites spent wandering in the desert.

Planting the seed

Lent is a great time to start making regular Bible reading a practice for your family. You can choose a particular book to read together during Lent or read through a variety of stories. Lent is a time to prepare ourselves to understand the death and resurrection of Christ, and so having a regular time of reading and conversation about the Bible with children during Lent will be the best thing to help them prepare and practise for the more intense conversations you can have about Holy Week (see items 61–64).

Feeding the soil

Congregations often use the season of Lent to add extra worship or study activities for the community. Whatever they may be, be sure to be mindful of the ways children are included in those activities. Lent can be a very heavy and 'adult' season.

As an adult I appreciate contemplative worship during the season of Lent, a practice that by its very nature can be a struggle for children who find it hard to be 'still' for that long. So to help them stay connected during contemplative worship, add elements to the service that will be sure to engage them. Taizé-style singing is very easy for children to pick up and join in. Candle lighting, while needing adult assistance, is always a highlight for children. Even providing Lenten journals and coloured pencils in worship space can encourage purposeful doodling and colouring during the service.[1]

---

[1] My friend the Revd Theresa Cho has created some amazing resources and ideas for including children in these kinds of interactive and contemplative inter-generational worship experiences. You can find links to a variety of services and ideas on her blog – <www.theresaecho.com>.

Watching them grow

As students get older they are ready to think seriously about what prayer practices resonate with their place on their journey of faith.

- How does Jesus teach us to pray?
- How does Jesus show us how to pray?
- Does everyone need to practise their faith in the same way?
- Do different spiritual practices fit better with different personalities?
- What does it mean when we experience seasons of doubt and struggle in our faith?
- Is this a sign of failure or lack of faith?
- How do we reconnect?
- How do we learn from our questions and our wilderness experiences?

83 Easter

Easter is the 50-day celebration of the resurrection of Jesus Christ. Throughout several weeks a congregation using the Revised Common Lectionary in worship will move through multiple stories of Jesus' appearances to his disciples to celebrate the resurrection. This season is marked by the colour white.

Planting the seed

Helping children get the most out of their time in worship starts before you even get to church on Sunday. If your church publicizes the Scripture passages that will be read and preached on each week, start a tradition of reading those assigned passages at home with children *before* Sunday morning. Talk together about them:

- What do you think this passage is teaching us about God?
- What does it teach us about ourselves?
- What good news does this story have for our church community?
- How does this passage help us celebrate this particular season?

The season of Easter is a lovely time to start this practice, especially in a community that uses a lectionary. On Easter Sunday we hear the stories of the first appearances of Jesus but on the following Sundays we hear many additional Gospel stories of Jesus appearing to the disciples: to Thomas (John 20.24–31); to two disciples on the road to Emmaus (Luke 24.13–35); to a group of disciples on the beach (John 21).

Feeding the soil

I can remember vividly as a child singing the Avery and Marsh song 'Every Morning is Easter Morning'. For some reason the sentiment of this song really stuck with me even as a child. The idea that we are living in a perpetual Easter and that as Christians we are people of the resurrection was meaningful to me.

Explain to children that every Sunday – no matter the season – is an Easter Sunday. That is why we don't count the Sundays in Lent among the 40 days – because they are weekly Easter respites. Every Sunday is the Lord's Sunday and an occasion to celebrate the resurrection. Making this kind of language a regular part of how we talk to children about the importance of Sunday – the Lord's Day – can go a long way to instilling this Easter identity in them as well.

Watching them grow

The resurrection of Christ is one of the fundamental tenets of Christian faith. The belief not just that Jesus died to save us from our sins but that he defeated death itself speaks to the power of God over sin and the hope of our own resurrection in Christ when we die. And yet as integral as this belief is to our life of faith, there is something about it that is essentially unbelievable. Young people need to have space to ask questions about the resurrection that allow them to sit in a place of unbelief for a while. There are any number of theories of what might have happened to Jesus' body after his death that are much more plausible than resurrection.

- What if it never happened?
- How do we answer those who question our faith and our tradition?
- What does it mean to be a Christian who struggles to believe?
- Is there a place in the church for those who are still trying to understand who Jesus Christ is for them?
- How do we encourage one another while also being grace-filled with each other?

84 Pentecost

Pentecost immediately follows the 50 days of Easter, kicked off by a celebration of the coming of the Holy Spirit to the disciples in the book of Acts (see item 76 for a larger description). We mark this season with the colour red and frequently refer to it as the birthday of the Church.

Planting the seed

As we celebrate the birthday of the Church we can talk to our children about the gifts not just that they are able to give themselves to the community but the gifts they receive or that your family receives from the community. Talk with them about the times when people from your church family have reached out to you to offer help, a meal, encouragement or even just friendship.

- How can your family make sure to thank those people regularly?
- Is there a way that your child might be sure to express thanks?

When my son was born a couple of women in our church made him a beautiful quilt, which he still uses on his bed to this day. Every so often I would remind him who made it for him, and inevitably, soon after that, I would overhear him saying thank you to one of the women at church, wholly unprompted. Yes, we strive to teach our children the importance of reaching out to help others, but it is just as important to instil in them the willingness to be helped by others and to show gratitude for the community's support of them.

Feeding the soil

In my particular tradition we focus a great deal on the role of the Holy Spirit, not just in inspiring the original writing of Scripture but in our hearing and interpreting it today as a community and as individuals. This means that in our worship life we regularly pray a prayer of illumination to remind ourselves to be led by the Spirit in our reading and hearing of the Word.

In children's classes we often begin/end our time together with prayer as a way to ask for God's presence among us as we meet, and God's blessing on us in our leaving. Why not help children remember to rely on the power of the Holy Spirit when you are reading the Bible together in class? Writing or choosing a simple prayer for illumination for the classroom can be a way of reminding children of the sacredness of reading Scripture in community and of God's presence with them when they try to understand it in class. Here is one such prayer – simple, and one of my favourites:

Guide us, O God, by your Word and Spirit,
that in your light we may see light,
in your truth find freedom,
and in your will discover your peace;
through Jesus Christ our Lord. Amen[2]

Watching them grow

I mentioned in the last chapter that I like to read 1 Corinthians 12 with my confirmation students to help them understand the gifts that are given to the community. This passage ends with a list from Paul of some of the gifts of the Spirit that we are called to celebrate, including teaching, healing, speaking in tongues, interpreting tongues, prophesy and leadership. Older teenagers are ready to wrestle with this very first-century list of gifts.

- Why in so many churches do we no longer celebrate the gift of tongues?
- When did it become strange to our Christian practice and faith?
- Where do we listen for prophets in our communities?
- Do we only recognize gifts that are part of our experience?
- Can we recognize legitimacy in Christian traditions that still focus on these gifts when we do not?

85 Ordinary Time

And then there is Ordinary Time. Marked by green, Ordinary Time fills the weeks between seasons. Sometimes the season between Christmas and Lent is considered 'ordinary', though others refer to those weeks as the season of Epiphany. Most often Ordinary Time lasts through the summer and autumn from Pentecost to Advent.

Planting the seed

One of the most regular conversations that we all have with our children is about why every single week, when every part of our brain and body wants to sleep in, we get up, shower, get dressed and go to church. It isn't a holiday; there is nothing that our family has agreed to 'do' at church that day; grandparents are not in town; there is no special speaker or preacher and no meeting to attend. Yet we still go to church.

---

[2] *Book of Common Worship* (Louisville, KY: Westminster John Knox Press, 1994). Used by kind permission.

The ordinary days are the days when we need the community. The ordinary days are when it's easiest to forget that we are part of something bigger than ourselves. These are the days when nothing else might remind us and our families of who and whose we are if we don't take the time and effort to remind each other. But the ordinary days are also the ones when we have time to build relationships, sit in worship in the quiet that is present when there is nothing extraordinary going on besides the people of God all deciding to be together that day to worship God.

Feeding the soil

One of the things that we love to do with children and young people is to introduce them to the heroes of faith. This is often how we describe characters from the Bible and other leaders throughout the history of the Church. From Abraham to Martin Luther King, Jr. we use these heroes to teach children how a faithful person responds to the call of God. But chances are we are not – and they are not – all Abrahams and Kings, so what children really need is a relationship with and a connection to the ordinary Christians in their lives who can show them what an ordinary life of faith is all about.

Create these relationships through intentional mentorships and prayer partnerships between adults and children and young people in your congregation. In my tradition, confirmation often necessitates the creation of those relationships, but starting earlier, even at five or six years old, can help children connect with the community in a more intentional way.

Watching them grow

What does it mean for worship and church participation to be an ordinary part of our life – and our life of faith? A generation before ours, the church was one of the primary communities for families. There are so many other things that pull us away from the church community. How do we recapture that connection?

86 Basic worship practices

While children shouldn't be expected always to understand the nuances or theology behind particular worship practices, they should come to feel comfortable participating in the worship life of the community. They should be taught to find their way through a church bulletin or prayer book. They should know when you normally stand up and when you sit down. They should know the flow of the service: what comes first, middle and last.

Planting the seed

One of the primary complaints that I hear from parents about worshipping with their children is that they make too much noise, distracting all of the adults around them. I will allow that this is sometimes is the case. But we put ourselves in this situation when we expect that without any instructions, explanations or encouragement children will simply want to sit quietly in an uncomfortable pew for an hour. Of course they don't. I don't either. It is only because I understand what is happening around me, what to anticipate next and how I am expected to respond that I as an adult get anything out of worship.

As my son has grown, our time in worship has changed as well. When he was very young I thought that I would never have a peaceful and personal moment in worship again, but now that he is ten years old things have significantly improved. I attribute that in no small part to all of the awkward, slightly disruptive and unfulfilling moments we had in the pew together when I explained what was going on, told him how he needed to respond and interpreted what the people around him were doing.

My advice on having conversations with children about worship is that the best and most fruitful conversations happen in the midst of worship. In my experience, if people are distracted by parents and children worshiping together they are likely to find a quieter spot the following Sunday. But it is also my experience that these sounds and distractions can be celebrated by a church as a sign of growth and new life.

Feeding the soil

No matter how many classes on worship practices a child might attend, the most effective way to teach them how to worship is to include them in the regular worship life of a congregation. The best worship educators you have in your congregation are parents, and so the most effective way to use class time is to educate *parents* on the hows and whys of worship, to ensure them continually that their children are welcome in worship and to teach non-parents how to foster a welcoming community for children and families who are anxious about disrupting other people in worship.

Watching them grow

When an older student is steeped in the 'what' and 'how' of worship, we can spend time encouraging their 'whys'.

- Why do we sing so many songs?
- Who gets to pick the songs?
- Why do I have to say a prayer of confession that makes me confess sins I didn't do that week?
- Why is the sermon so long?
- Who decides when we have Communion?
- Why do I have to shake hands and pass the peace with strangers around me?
- Why do the children leave in the middle of the service?
- Why is there such a long prayer at the end?

Most importantly, we can spend time considering the purpose of Christian worship: what we bring to it and what we get out of it.

87 Your family's religious background

I have heard my fair share of stories about people's religious journeys – the ways the church in which they were raised shaped their religious experience both positively and negatively, the ways their parents and grandparents guided their faith or hindered it, the ways they moved through different phases of their own faith, both the mountain tops and the valleys. While it seems like these are the stories we are supposed to tell our pastors or other religious leaders, they are also stories we need to tell our children regularly.

Planting the seed

Whenever we make a visit back to my home and my home congregation, I always take a moment to remind my son of the significance of that place in my faith journey. Within the confines of one sanctuary I can walk him to the spot where I was baptized, where I knelt to be confirmed, where I stood with my husband at our wedding, even where my friends and I hid when we played hide and seek at church overnights.

Even if you are not able to take your children on this kind of religious memory tour, you can still be sharing stories with them about growing up inside or outside the church. Ask grandparents and other relatives to share their stories as well, to give children a fuller picture of the traditions and the places from which they came. Tell them where you have been on your journey and why you have chosen your current congregation as the place where they will grow into faith.

Feeding the soil

Some of the best education moments we can create for children are inter-generational. When we teach children and parents together, each child has an adult conversation partner with them, and we can nurture and practise the kinds of conversations we would hope families are having at home in a more directed setting.

Gather families together at tables with art materials, such as large sheets of paper, coloured markers, pencils and crayons, and ask them to create a family tree together. Parents could be encouraged ahead of time to bring family photos with them to help tell the stories of older family members. As each generation is added, have parents tell the stories of these branches of the family, their religious traditions and even the lessons that parents might have learnt from them. If you do this activity at a gathering for all of your church families, ask each family to bring a food to share that is special to their family.

Watching them grow

If students are being confirmed in the same tradition as family members before them, what does it mean to carry on a faith that was handed down to them? If they are being confirmed in a new tradition, it is essential for them to understand how and why that change was made – what was it about this new tradition that was meaningful to their parents or grandparents, and how might it be important to them? Students who do not come from a religious background need to understand what motivated their family to join a church and how they are part of a new tradition.

88 How parents (grandparents) volunteer or lead in the church

I am pretty sure students know that their parents do things at church. But often they don't understand the implications of their parents' involvement, whether as an elder or deacon, a teacher, a cooker of meals for the homeless shelter, a member of a search committee, an organizer of a capital campaign or even as the person we call when the toilets won't flush.

Planting the seed

As a pastor there are many nights when I rush from the dinner table to attend an evening meeting at my church. Yes, sometimes meetings are held during the day, but in a world where most people are volunteers, most meetings happen at night. When my son was younger I am not sure how often I told him what my meeting was about, but I know I often reminded him I was going to a meeting with the men and women who were the church leaders, to help them make decisions about the community.

These conversations should not just be happening between pastors and their children but within all families where parents are giving their time and talents to their faith community. While not all the work we do as volunteers for the church is exciting, it is all important. When you explain to children about the ways you are involved at church, make sure always to talk about two things: first, why you think the work is important – maybe important to the community or important to you; second, why you have been asked or why you volunteered to do this work. This helps children understand that there are many kinds of gifts that we are given by God and that each of us has something unique – unique skills or unique experiences – that can be contributed to the community.

Feeding the soil

I have many childhood memories of my church and my church community, but some of the most vivid are of helping my mother, waiting for my mother or even watching my mother volunteer at church.

Each time your church asks parents to be a part of the life of the congregation, whether through giving of time, talents or leadership, you should also ask how the church is including their family in this work.

- Is it possible to offer childcare when meetings are held so that parents can be more flexible in their availability?
- Are there ways to include children in the work that needs to be done?
- Is there simply grace enough to allow children to be with their parents and watch them in action?

Some of my favourite moments would come when children tagged along with parents to the church during the week – especially when I was not involved in that particular project. It gave me as their pastor time to have longer conversations with children than I ever had on Sunday mornings. I always made sure to explain to them what their parents were doing for the church that day and telling them how much I appreciated their gifts.

Watching them grow

A vital skill for students to gain as they grow into their faith is how actually to *be* a member of a congregation. But talking about it in a class is not really how they are going to learn. They are going to learn how to be a member of their congregation by watching their parents and grandparents be members of a congregation – for better or for worse.

As young people get older they can be given opportunities to serve alongside adults in the congregation, to be a part of decision-making for different aspects of the life of the community, and to share their voice and experiences with their church family. Put them in places where they can watch the work of the church being done and they will consider where their gifts might best be used, and even where they are *not* feeling called to serve. I used to take students with me on visits to elderly members of our congregation, and once on the drive back to church I had a young man confess that he would never be able to do this kind of ministry on his own. This led to a wonderful conversation about what gifts he did see in himself and how he wanted to serve the church in different ways. Young people learn by doing, and the church should be a place where we invite them in with grace to try out as many ways of service and leadership as there are, to help them discern how best to live out their faith and commitment to the Christian community as they live into an identity as adult members of the church.

89 Communion practices

While I believe that the best way to teach children about Communion is actually to allow them to participate in the sacrament, in many traditions (including some parts of my own) it is the practice to wait until an age of understanding (or even until confirmation) before a child/young person is welcomed to the Communion table.

Regardless of whether or not children are welcomed at your Communion table, it is essential to teach them the significance of the sacrament and the role it serves in the community to gather the people together, to give thanks for the saving work of God through Christ and to bring renewal and sustenance to the community so that it might work for Christ in the world.

Planting the seed

No matter what your tradition, it is likely that your community's celebration of Communion includes the following elements:

- an invitation to the table;
- a prayer of thanksgiving;
- a remembrance of the words Jesus spoke at the Last Supper – the words of institution;
- a sharing of the elements among the community;
- a prayer after all have been served.

Talk with children about how these rhythms of Communion are very similar to the meals we share around our tables at home:

- We are called to gather at the table.
- We give thanks for the food before us.
- We recall and recount for each other the experiences we have had that day.
- We share in the meal together.

As you sit in worship with your child during the sacrament, point out all the movements of the liturgy as they are happening. Mealtime in the home is always a time of instruction in manners, conversation, sharing, and shared responsibility; mealtime in worship is no different.

Feeding the soil

Primarily at the request of families who were composed of blended Christian traditions, I created an inter-generational workshop to help parents and children learn about Communion together. Children and parents came together for the evening, and we moved through interactive stations that facilitated their conversations as family groups. We would start seated on the floor around a low table to talk about the Last Supper. Then I provided a wide selection of artistic depictions of the Last Supper and asked each person to select the one they liked the most. Families sat to talk about what they saw in each picture and what they liked about it. We studied – again in family groups – other feeding stories from both the Old and New Testaments, and brainstormed ways they help us think about the Communion meal. We spent time talking about our mealtime at home, and children drew images of their family table. Finally we gathered in the sanctuary to touch, feel and taste the Communion elements and talk about the physical logistics of sharing Communion.

Watching them grow

I teach older students Communion the same way I do baptism. We hold our own Communion service, with two of the students celebrating at the table, leading their small congregation, breaking the bread, pouring the wine and sharing the feast with one another.

With their leadership we can talk about all the moments and gestures they recall – why we do them and what they mean.

- Who has given the invitation?
- How do we retell the story of the Last Supper?
- Who is welcomed to share in the feast together?

While they may have tasted the bread and the juice for themselves many times before, it tastes just a little sweeter when they have done it for themselves and with each other.

90 Baptismal practices

Because confirmation is in essence a confirming of a student's baptism, helping them seriously reflect on the sacrament of baptism is meaningful as they mature in their faith. Most likely students will not come with a fully fleshed-out baptismal theology, but even as children they should be able to describe what happens in worship when someone is baptized.

Planting the seed

One of my son's favourite pages in his baby book is the page with photos from the day of his baptism. At six months he obviously was not old enough to remember it for himself, and yet as he got older he witnessed multiple baptisms of infants born after him. I think it is fascinating for him to see a picture of himself doing something he has seen done for others first-hand.

In our particular baptismal liturgy we always end the theological statement on baptism with the phrase, 'Let us remember with joy our own baptism'. People tend to baulk at that statement because as members of a primarily infant baptism tradition hardly anyone actually remembers their own baptism. The sentiment of the statement, though, really means that we are to remember with joy our own identity as baptized children of God each time we witness the baptism of another.

Our children will remember and connect with their baptismal identity by having conversations with you as parents about your decision to have them baptized and what you did to celebrate that day as a family. Each time you watch a baptism with your children, remind them that your family did the same for them.

Feeding the soil

In my Presbyterian tradition we take special care during baptism to focus on promises made by the community to the child: promises to welcome them into the family of faith and to teach and nurture them in the faith. Typically these promises are part of the formal liturgy as the congregation stands and affirms their responsibility in the child's life.

In the congregation I served, my colleague in pastoral leadership had also instituted another tradition to help the community remember the weight of these promises. After the baptism we would carry the child through the sanctuary so that the congregation could see the baby up close. During that time we would remind them of the ways this child would become a part of the community and the ways the community would be an important part of the child's life. And then we would stop and physically hand the child to a member of the congregation, visibly enacting the welcoming arms of the church.

It is such a simple act and yet it is one of the things I heard people talk about all the time when it came to the ways the entire church has committed itself to the Christian nurture of children. They have held these children in their own arms, they have welcomed them into the family of faith and they are committed to walk with them throughout their lives.

Watching them grow

I like to teach the meaning of baptism with older students by play-acting a baptism. The students take on different roles in the sacrament: pastor, parents, elder, congregation and children.

By walking through the statements of Scripture, the promises made by parents and members of the church, the beautiful prayer said over the water, the affirmation of faith and the actual act of baptizing, we can explore the deeper meanings of the sacrament. We move beyond that sweet moment students have seen in pictures from when they were young to what it will mean for them to make those same promises for others as adult members of the church.

14

The body of Christ

————•◦•————

In Pittsburgh, Pennsylvania I grew up in a suburb that contained a large Roman Catholic community. As a little Presbyterian girl I knew that my experience of Christianity was different but I wasn't exactly sure how. It wasn't unusual for some of my Catholic friends to ask me if Presbyterians were even Christians. As a third grader I didn't know how to answer that question convincingly. It had never crossed my mind that someone would think I wasn't actually a Christian. It was also not unusual for me to be invited to mass to celebrate a friend's first Communion or other ritual moment in the life of their church. In those moments I could feel the difference in our traditions without language to describe what they were.

At the very same time, growing up in south-western Pennsylvania meant that I was growing up Presbyterian in an incredibly dense population of Presbyterians. Presbyterian liturgy, theology, biblical interpretation, social witness and church governance were so much the air I breathed that I could not have articulated to anyone how they were different from any other form of Protestantism, let alone Christianity. It wasn't until I was in seminary that I even learned what makes the Presbyterian tradition uniquely different from any other Christian tradition.

Children and younger teenagers may not be able to articulate the nuanced distinctions between different Christian denominations but they should have an understanding that there are some things that are foundational to Christian faith, and that built upon that foundation are different ways of practising that faith. As they get older and choose to be a member of one particular Christian denomination, it should be a choice they are making intentionally. Instilling in children a larger understanding of their place in the body of Christ will help them claim it for themselves when they are older.

91 The Apostles' Creed

The Apostles' Creed, written in the fourth century, articulates the basics of Christian faith affirmed by the vast majority of Christian denominations. While children may not be able to parse the sophisticated theology it strives to simplify, its language should be a part of their religious vocabulary.

> I believe in God, the Father almighty, creator of heaven and earth.
>
> I believe in Jesus Christ, his only Son, our Lord, who was conceived by the Holy Spirit, born of the Virgin Mary, suffered under Pontius Pilate, was crucified, died, and was buried; he descended to the dead. On the third day he rose again; he ascended into heaven, he is seated at the right hand of the Father, and he will come to judge the living and the dead.
>
> I believe in the Holy Spirit, the holy catholic Church, the communion of saints, the forgiveness of sins, the resurrection of the body, and the life everlasting.
>
> Amen.[1]

Planting the seed

When we worship together with children we are showing them by example how one fully participates in the liturgy and movements of community worship. Even though my son is old enough to have his own bulletin/order of service, I still like to share one with him. This means that when we are praying or responding in worship our heads and voices are close together. It becomes a moment of joint worship between us. I try to do this when we speak the words of the creed together, first because I want him to keep up and follow along, making sure he is not blandly reciting words that have little meaning to him; second because I want to ensure he hears my voice speaking these same words. As he grows in his faith and explores the meaning of the creed for himself, I want him sometimes to hear the words in my voice, knowing that this essential Christian faith is something he has inherited from his parents.

Even doing these simple things with our children provides opportunities to talk about what it is we believe and why. There have been

[1] *Common Worship: Services and Prayers for the Church of England* (London: Church House Publishing, 2000), p. 141. Copyright © ELLC 1988. Reproduced by kind permission.

numerous times when my son has whispered a question to me about the creed in worship after we have read it together. If we had not recited it together in that moment both the question and the conversation would have been lost.

Feeding the soil

It goes without saying that children who recite the creed in worship will come to know the creed. But even when children know *what* to do in worship, it doesn't always mean they know *why* it is done. If any creed – not just the Apostles' Creed – is a regular part of your liturgy, be sure those leading worship take the time to explain why it is we make this public declaration together as a community of faith.

Watching them grow

When I first started preparing students for confirmation, memorizing the Apostles' Creed was one of the major tasks they were to accomplish. After a few years I stopped doing it, primarily because it was a struggle to get those who were either not inclined or able to do so to complete the assignment. Too much class time was wasted on watching students struggle through the recitation. Instead, class time was much more effectively invested having a real conversation about the creed itself.

One of the questions that always comes up – for students and adults – is what we mean by the Holy Catholic Church. What does it mean to believe in the Church universal (which is the definition of 'catholic' with a little 'c') – a Church that is bigger than their own congregation, bigger than their own denomination, bigger than even the churches and Christians who live today. To recite this creed means to affirm a belief in a Church that is the body of Christ, including those who have come before us and those who will carry on the faith after we are gone. This is the faith and the Church in which they are also confirmed.

Four major branches of the Church universal

The next four items on this list include four of the major branches of the body of Christ. They are included on this list as a means of encouraging children to have the broadest understanding of the global Church. As I mentioned at the start of this chapter, I would in no way expect children to be able to articulate the specific differences between these traditions. But these are traditions that are worth recognizing. Parents, teachers and pastors should take the time to acknowledge the differences and give thanks for the diversity within the body of Christ.

Obviously I am encouraging an open and appreciative model when it comes to talking with children about ecumenical relationships. And yet the history of the Church – and the reason there are so many branches and denominations – is coloured with debates, discord and division. Just like in our own families, sometimes there are fights, separations and brokenness. We remind children and ourselves that it is Christ's hope that some day these divisions will be no more.

Under each branch below I have simply put what I choose to high-light from each tradition when I teach students about these different parts of the family of faith. These are by no means an exhaustive summary of each and should simply serve as a reminder or a refresher for those who are looking for simple ways to talk about these trad-itions with children.

92 Roman Catholic

While there was a time when there was only one Church, it certainly was not without diversity and division. Today's Roman Catholic Church continues to represent that Church and tradition that is rooted in the leadership of the Roman Catholic Pope. When I talk to students about the Catholic Church, I highlight the value of tradition, of apostolic succession and of the monastic movement. I always take a moment to talk about saints, what it means to be a saint and how we can experience God through the service and faith of others.

93 Orthodox

A major break in the Church came in the eleventh century over theological debates about the nature of the Trinity and the work of the Holy Spirit, splitting the Church geographically between Eastern and Western. Today there is no single Orthodox Church, but several that developed in different parts of the world. This would include Greek Orthodox, Russian Orthodox and Coptic (Egyptian) Orthodox, just to name a few. One of the things I like to highlight for students when talking about the Eastern Orthodox Church is their tradition of incorporating art into religious space and their prolific use of icons. Even though it is not a part of my tradition, I can model for students – and my son – an appreciation of the art form and its beauty in depicting a variety of images from Scripture and church history in such striking ways.

94 Anglican

During the reign of Henry VIII in England (1509–47), disputes between the King and the Roman Catholic Pope led to a significant break from the Church in Rome and the creation of what became the Church of England (Anglican Church). The Anglican tradition falls in a middle place between the Roman Catholic and Reformed Protestant traditions – an affirmation of the sacraments and clerical orders in tandem with the authority of Scripture. The Anglican Reformation eventually led to the development of the Puritan move-ment and the Methodist Church. When I talk with students about the gifts of the Anglican Church, we always look at the beauty that can be found in liturgy and how it shapes our belief, worship and community life together.

95 Protestant

Protestants are a broad category of churches within a particular tradition that began in the sixteenth century as a variety of leaders within the Roman Catholic Church began to 'protest' its governance *and* theology. From this movement came Presbyterians and Lutherans, to name just two. While each separate Protestant denomination has its own distinctive ways of articulating Christian faith, for the most part they highlight the authority of Scripture over church law, the leadership of non-ordained – lay – people within the church and the ability of all Christians to petition and confess to God through Christ without the need for a priest – which is where we get the doctrine of the priesthood of all believers.

Planting the seed

I am part of an ecumenical family. While I have been a Presbyterian all of my life, my husband was raised Mennonite and can trace his

Anabaptist roots back several generations. This means we have conversations at home with our son all the time about different ways to be Christian, and encourage him to understand the different traditions that make up his family. While we are unique in the ways we are trying to raise him to understand himself as fully a part of both traditions, it is actually very common in my North American context for families to have parents who were raised in different Christian traditions choose one over the other when they get married and have children. In item 87 I talked about how we should be talking with children about our family's religious background and traditions. Describe to children what you as a parent changed in your religious practice when you moved from one part of the Christian family to another.

When we have conversations with children about sacraments, the Bible, ordained service in the church or any number of things on which Christians differ, it is inevitable that they will sometimes offer up alternative understandings of each. It is also highly probable that they will suggest an alternative that accurately represents the tenets of a different branch of the Christian Church. Tell them that there are some Christians who actually believe that to be true, but that in your branch of the faith something different is believed. And then spend the time sharing your belief with them. While these are the kinds of moments that can instil anxiety in parents who worry that they don't know enough to teach children about their faith, they can also teach children how to find out more about what their specific church believes.

Feeding the soil

As a pastor it is always one of my goals to try to instil in children and young people an appreciation for their heritage as Presbyterians. I mentioned earlier that as a child I could have explained what we believed as a church but not how that was any different from any other church. So when teaching in my congregation something unique about our Presbyterian tradition I start with, 'As Presbyterians we believe . . .', but when I am teaching something that fits with a variety of Christian traditions I start with, 'As Christians we believe . . .'

As much as I try to highlight for children and young people the unique qualities of our own tradition, I also never hesitate to share with them the things I valued from others. This isn't limited to practices or pillars of faith but also the work other churches do in areas of social service or relief. Even though our own Presbyterian denomination does wonderful work when disasters strike around the world, one school year our children solicited donations for Mennonite Central Committee relief kits and learned more about the ways MCC works around the world. Even in this simple act of ecumenism our children were learning that we have brother and sister Christians outside of our tradition with whom we work together in partnership.

Watching them grow

What does it mean not just to affirm the essentials of Christianity but to do so within a specific and historic context? I would never expect teenagers to think they could make a once in a lifetime decision – at age 14 – about what kind of church they wanted to be a part of and what kind of Christian they wanted to be. But when it comes to this first of many moments when they will choose to root themselves in a specific community, they should do so understanding the uniqueness, the struggles and the expectations of that community.

Many of my colleagues who also teach confirmation students have shared with me that one of the most beneficial journeys they take students on during this year of preparation is through the diversity that is the body of Christ. It is only when students experience a different way of being Christian that they can look with fresh eyes on their own tradition. When we start teaching children about this kind of diversity and exposing them to the greater Christian community when they are young, the preparation for confirmation can been even more meaningful, their minds and hearts can be more open to experiencing different models of Christian expression and they can discover a renewed identity in their own church.

15

World religions

———•◦•———

I mentioned in the previous chapter that my husband and I were raised in different Christian traditions, making us an ecumenical family – a blending of both the Reformed and Anabaptist traditions. But at the same time that I was entering the ministry around 2002, my older brother began the process of taking his vows as a Theravada Buddhist monk, which also makes us an inter-religious family.

This means that our son has never seen his uncle in western-style clothing or known him as anything but Uncle Bhante – a Pali word meaning 'venerable'. Being inter-religious was nothing we ever had to introduce him to. It is his only world view.

Added to this is the fact that for our son's third- and fourth-grade years we lived in the centre of Cairo, Egypt – the city of 1,000 minarets. Daily life cycled around the audible calls to prayer five times a day, restrictions on food and clothing, and unfamiliar holidays we watched our neighbours celebrate.

While these circumstances have given us unique opportunities to allow him to understand our Christian traditions in contrast with other religions, I would hope that even without both of these unique experiences we still would have taken the time to help him understand the role of Christianity in the larger landscape of global religions.

Of all the conversations we have together with our son about faith, his questions about other religions are the ones that repeat most often. When my son asks again and again about what it means to be a different religion, I choose to believe that he is not so much interested in whatever religion he is asking about that day as he is in understanding why we have chosen ours.

As students get older we can spend more time with them exploring world religions. But just as crucial is talking about what it means to be a Christian in the world today, and that inevitably means talking about how we as Christians interact with other religions.

Instinctively I want to teach them to respect and even appreciate other faith traditions. And yet most young people these days have a decidedly postmodern perspective on the world, which means they are already comfortable with differences and differences of opinion. They don't usually need me to teach them respect; they need to hear from me – just as my son does – why it is I have chosen, and why they may choose, to be a Christian amid a diverse religious landscape.

Certainly there are moments when misperceptions and prejudices about other religions need to be named and corrected in class. Not all young people are postmodern, and not all of them are being raised in homes that would welcome open conversations about other religions.

Below I have highlighted just a few of the primary distinctions of five world religions. I am not a scholar of any of them and these summaries should only be used as a jumping-off point or a basic orientation to each tradition. There are some wonderful resources available online and in print to help children learn even more about each.

96 Christianity

Christianity is a global religion that has the same kind of geographic and historical elements to it that we often use to define other world religions. At the most basic, students should have a sense that Christianity began in the first century in Palestine and soon spread throughout the Middle East and into Northern Africa and Europe. They should understand that Christianity is one of the three primary monotheistic religions. They should also understand that of the major world religions, Christianity is the only one that believes in the incarnation of God in human form.

97 Islam

I started teaching my first confirmation class in the autumn of 2002, right around the first anniversary of September 11th. Of all the world religions, this is the one that needs the most correction or explanation for students. Frequently students would come to class with misperceptions or even just false information that they had gleaned from a variety of sources. So while there is a lot that I hope students don't come knowing – or thinking they know – about Islam, here are the things that they should know. They should know that Islam is a monotheistic religion, founded by the prophet Mohamed. They should know that Muslims trace their ancestral heritage to Abraham and that their Scripture is the Qur'an. They should also know that while Islam started in the Middle East, there are Muslims living all over the world.

98 Judaism

For many years part of our confirmation class included a visit to a local synagogue for Friday evening worship. It was always a meaningful experience. Judaism is one of the hardest of the world religions for students to wrap their heads around, I believe, because it is so closely connected to our heritage as Christians – with one significant difference. Students need to understand that Christians and Jews share the tradition of the Old Testament, that the primary characters of the Old Testament would all be considered Jewish – though this is an oversimplification of the development of the history of Israel and the faith of the Israelites – and most importantly that Jesus and his disciples were Jewish.

99 Sikhism

Sikhism is the fifth-largest world religion and the youngest of the five listed here. It developed in the fifteenth century, based on the teachings of a collection of Sikh gurus. Two primary tenets of Sikhism focus on the oneness of God and the equality of human beings. Sikhs are known for their priority for service to God and the community, their commitment to certain prohibitions such as cutting of their hair or drinking of alcohol, but also their rejection of any kind of priestly/ordained ministry and what they would characterize as blind rituals.

100 Hinduism

Hinduism may be even harder to quantify for children and young people, but here are some of the basics they should be able to grasp.

Hinduism is the ancient religion of India and the root tradition of Buddhism. Hinduism is not a monotheistic religion. A variety of different traditions and gods make up a pantheon of possibilities when it comes to how one practises Hinduism. Hinduism is also where we find the origin of the concept of reincarnation.

Planting the seed

I have already talked about having conversations with our son with a Buddhist uncle and living in a Muslim majority culture, but how do we talk to children about other religions when it takes our effort and initiative to engage them in a topic they may not have considered before?

There are several opportunities to spark conversations with children in our day-to-day lives. The first is through architecture. Make sure to point out to children when you pass or are near a place of worship or gathering for a different faith tradition. Stop together to notice the temple, synagogue or mosque in your neighbourhood. What symbols or architectural features help us recognize it? What signs do we see that this is a sacred place?

Clothing is another way to help start conversations. While not all people who practise any given religion choose to wear particular clothing that sets them apart from others, quite often they do. How do we react when we see people dressed differently from the way we would expect? Why are there different expectations about women's clothing and headwear than men's? Do the leaders of these different traditions dress differently from their congregation?

Inevitably in a 24-hour global news cycle, children are also going to hear about the ways different religions are wrapped up in geo-politics: news of violence in the Middle East, demonstrations against religious and cultural restrictions in South East Asia, hate crimes in our own cities and towns. These are also moments to talk with children about differences in religion, to remind them that just because an individual claims to be part of a particular faith tradition, this does not mean they are representative of the full diversity within that tradition or even the basic teachings of that religion.

Feeding the soil

Throughout this book I have given ideas about how to take advantage of different moments in the life of the congregation to help prepare children for the rite of passage that is their choice to be confirmed as a disciple of Jesus Christ and as a member of a particular congregation.

While there are many ways congregations can help children become more informed about the religions of the world, whether through curriculum or larger cooperative activities in the community, I believe that this topic of inter-religious dialogue is the perfect example of how we as a community need to continue to nurture the growing faith of students even after their confirmation year.

Christian education beyond confirmation is all about encouraging students to learn more about the implications of living as a Christian in the world. How are the decisions I make at home or at school, with my friends or family and some day in my adult life, affected by my Christian faith? I call these the 'So what?' conversations. So you have decided to be confirmed as an adult Christian and a member of a specific community of faith. So what? How does that mean your life is different or unique? Older students are primed and ready to explore the larger world of religion in both the classroom and the community.

Using the time between confirmation and graduation to encourage students to learn more about Christianity, the Bible, Christian ethics and how Christians live faithfully within a diverse religious landscape will help them make the often bumpy transition to an adult life of faith.

Watching them grow

There are several ways young people can make connections between their Christian faith and traditions and the experiences and beliefs of other world religions. For example, talking about the ways Muslims respect and care for the Qur'an can provide some perspective on how we treat our physical Bible. We can also touch on the ways the Christian Church has significantly persecuted the Jewish community over the past 2,000 years. What does it mean to be inheritors of that history as well?

When we talk about worshipping the same God as a Jew or a Muslim, we know that though we have different beliefs about God, we all refer to the same God, whom we believe to be the only God. When we as Christians relate to Hindus, we have to consider what it means for a faith to believe in an entirely different set of gods from us. Does that change our willingness to learn from that tradition?

Appendix 1
100 things for your child to know before confirmation – the complete list

―•◦•―

Bible basics

1 The Bible is made up of many different books with different authors
2 Much of the Bible comes from ancient oral tradition
3 The Old Testament is the story of the Israelite people
4 The New Testament is the story of the life of Jesus and the early Christians
5 There are many different modern translations of the Bible

The stories of Genesis and Exodus

6 Creation and other primeval stories (Gen. 1—11)
7 Noah's Ark (Gen. 6—9)
8 Abraham and Sarah (Gen. 12—23)
9 Isaac and Rebecca (Gen. 24—27)
10 Jacob and his sons (Gen. 28—50)
11 The birth of Moses (Exod. 2)
12 The call of Moses (Exod. 3)
13 The plagues (Exod. 7—12)
14 The Exodus (Exod. 12—13)
15 The wilderness experience (Exod. 15 and beyond)

The Ten Commandments (Exod. 2 and 32)

16 You shall worship God alone
17 You shall not make any idols of God
18 You shall not abuse the name of God
19 You shall keep the Sabbath holy
20 Honour your father and mother
21 You shall not murder
22 You shall not commit adultery

54 Water into wine (John 2.1–11)

55 The healing of the paralytic (Matt. 9.2–8; Mark 2.1–12; Luke 5.17–26)

Cherished stories of the New Testament

56 The call of the disciples (Matt. 4.18–22; Mark 1.16–20; Luke 5.1–11)

57 The Sermon on the Mount (Matt. 5.1—7.29)

58 The woman at the well (John 4.4–42)

59 Zacchaeus the tax collector (Luke 19.1–10)

60 Jesus' entry to Jerusalem (Palm Sunday) (Matt. 21.1–11; Mark 11.1–10; Luke 19.28–40; John 12.12–19)

61 Jesus cleanses the Temple (Matt. 21.12–17; Mark 11.15–19; Luke 19.45–48; John 2.12–25)

62 The Last Supper (Maundy Thursday) (Matt. 26.17–30; Mark 14.12–30; Luke 22.7–23)

63 Passion/crucifixion (Good Friday) (Matt. 26.36—27.61; Mark 14.32—15.47; Luke 22.39—23.56; John 18.1—19.42)

64 Resurrection (Easter) (Matt. 28; Mark 16; Luke 24.1–12; John 20.1–29)

65 Ascension (Mark 16.19–20; Luke 24.50–53; Acts 1.6–11)

The sayings and parables of Jesus

66 The Beatitudes (Matt. 5.3–11)

67 'Love your enemies and pray for those who persecute you' (Matt. 5.43–44)

68 'Do to others as you would have them do to you' (Matt. 7.12)

69 'Love the Lord your God . . . love your neighbour as yourself' (Matt. 22.37–40)

70 'For God so loved the world that he gave his only Son, so that everyone who believes in him may not perish but may have eternal life' (John 3.16)

71 The Good Samaritan (Luke 10.25–37)

72 The Lost Sheep and Coin (Luke 15.1–10)

73 Prodigal Son (Luke 15.11–32)

74 The Sower (Matt. 13.1–9)

75 The Mustard Seed (Matt. 13.31–32)

The Early Church

76 The gift of the Holy Spirit (Acts 2)

77 The conversion (call) of Paul (Acts 9)

78 The journeys and letters of Paul

79 The differences between Jews and Gentiles

80 The book of Revelation

Worship, sacraments and the life of the congregation

The body of Christ

World religions

Appendix 2
Further reading

———————•·•·•———————

Dorothy C. Bass (ed.), *Practicing Our Faith: A Way of Life for a Searching People*, 2nd edn (San Francisco, CA: Jossey-Bass, 2010).

Richard Friedman, *Who Wrote the Bible?* (Englewood Cliffs, NJ: Prentice Hall, 1987).

Donald Griggs, *The Bible from Scratch: The New Testament for Beginners* (Louisville, KY: Westminster John Knox, 2002).

Donald Griggs, *The Bible from Scratch: The Old Testament for Beginners* (Louisville, KY: Westminster John Knox, 2002).

Donald McKim, *A "Down and Dirty" Guide to Theology* (Louisville, KY: Westminster John Knox, 2011).

Stuart M. Matlins and Arthur J. Magida (eds), *How to be a Perfect Stranger: The Essential Religious Etiquette Handbook*, 6th edn (Woodstock, VT: SkyLight Paths, 2015).